Anger Management

Understanding Anger and Finding the Right Way to Deal with it

Dr. Mary Ann Martínez

Marcasa Books

This book contains information that is intended to help the readers be better informed. It is presented as general advice. Always consult your doctor for your individual needs. This book is not intended to be a substitute for the professional advice of a licensed therapist or licensed physician. The reader should consult with their healthcare professional in any matters relating to his/her mental health.

To all the men and women who have placed their trust in us; thank you for allowing us to walk with you on the road to recovery.

Dr. Mary Ann Martínez

CONTENTS

Introduction

We all get angry sometimes – that's normal human nature. All through the day, a lot of things happen that can really try our patience, but we usually try our best to control our anger before it does much harm.

Sometimes, it is mild irritation we feel because we've woken up late in the morning and missed breakfast before work; sometimes, we get slightly angrier because someone had just taken the last parking spot. However, sometimes our anger gets out of control, maybe when someone has broken something valuable we own and there's no way to retrieve it. There are times, when, in extreme anger, we lose ourselves and become someone entirely different. We say and do things we normally wouldn't, hurting others in the process.

While a little anger every now and then is a healthy outlet, excessive anger is harmful. Too much anger too often can harm us in a number of ways – mentally, emotionally, physically, spiritually, as well as financially. If this is the case, there is every need for some "Anger Management".

Anger Management refers to the healthy and scientific way of dealing with excess anger. Not by suppressing or hiding it so that we don't hurt anyone else, but by finding the right outlet. A number of studies and experiments have been conducted on this topic, making Anger Management a very important and effective part of psychology.

My book "Anger Management: *Understanding Anger and finding the right way to deal with it*" is not only about managing anger, but everything you need to know about this particular vice of us human beings. Reading about anger makes us understand it better, understand what happens to us when we get angry, why we do what we do (and say what we say), and more importantly, how we can manage it. I have included all these, and more topics, in this book.

I hope you will be able to find all the information you are looking for on anger and Anger Management here. I will consider myself successful if this book can help you in any way.

So get reading, and all the best!

Part One: Understanding Anger

Yes, anger is pretty common in human beings. We all have reasons to get angry, and we all – more or less – show anger when the situation demands it. So, what's the big deal?

The big deal is when anger gets out of hand, making us almost unrecognizable. Someone who was normal only a moment earlier, can become nasty and aggressive in an instant when angry. They can become abusive and violent, and in their anger, say and do something they will regret later. It's not just The Incredible Hulk who changes when angry; the average human beings can be in the same situation.

Why do we feel angry? When something doesn't go according to plan, when something happens that we don't like or don't want in our lives – that's when we feel anger. We get angry when we feel helpless in a situation, or when we feel threatened by someone or somebody. Why, we even feel angry at the simplest reasons when we are hungry or tired!

There are a lot of reasons for us to feel angry, and sometimes – it is actually a good thing. A little anger can be quite helpful in certain situations, but the problem arises when anger gets out of hand.

So what happens? Why do we get angry, and how does it affect us? How can too much anger harm our lives? What happens to our body when we get angry? How to tell if we are bordering on too much anger which will ultimately be harmful for us? These are the questions you will find the answer to in the first part of this book, so don't stop now!

What does Anger Mean?

Irritation, annoyance, resentment, animosity, rage, wrath – these are all variations of the same feeling, anger. We might be irritated by a person, resent someone, feel annoyed when it starts raining on the day we were planning a picnic, feel enraged when we break something precious. In the end, what we are feeling is anger.

There's nothing new to write about anger. We're all familiar with it, more or less. We all get angry at times, some of us more than others. Sometimes we hide it within ourselves, and sometimes we unleash it to the unsuspecting world. Some people are known to "have a temper" or "get angry easily" while others are always calm and quiet, barely showing their feelings.

Anger has lots of faces; sometimes, we can even frighten ourselves with the amount of hatred and rage we feel over something or someone. More often than not, we suppress our resentments, only to burst out later. Public burst-outs seem funny to the outsider, but they are humiliating to the people on the receiving end.

When some people, especially the type who is known to be highly strung, get angry, they tend to show violent streaks in themselves. This is how cases of domestic violence starts, when partners become abusive to their spouses, break belongings, threaten and hurt children and pets, etc. Bar fights and pub brawls – these usually happen when there is an angry person involved.

Can you define Anger?

It's actually very difficult to define anger. If you are asked to define what anger is, chances are you will start your answer with "situations that make you angry" or "what you feel like doing when you get angry". Most people would do the same when asked this question, because it is very difficult to explain this feeling accurately.

Because that's what anger is, an extremely powerful human emotion that causes us to momentarily forget ourselves and become someone else. When you are angry – very, very angry – you won't be able to recognize yourself; you will say and do things that are unlike you, only to feel remorse later. People who become violent and destructive in their anger rarely mean to behave the way they do, unless they have a history of abusive behavior.

Anger: A Complex Feeling

Another reason that it is difficult to define anger is because this is a complex emotion. We can understand why a person is feeling happy after a promotion, or when someone is sad after they have lost a loved one. We can understand emotions like joy, worry sorrow and hope easily; but anger in a person can seem completely ridiculous in another.

We can well understand the anger when we break a priceless antique by accident; but is it possible to comprehend why a person is screaming and cursing when they've run out of cigarettes at the middle of the night? Only the person who is feeling angry because of something so trivial can understand why they are angry, and no one else who is not in the same position.

Sometimes, it is hard to understand why we are angry about something, let alone understand the reasons behind someone else's emotions. Anger is, therefore, an incredibly complex emotion that varies from person to person, making it almost impossible to understand.

Anger: A Secondary Emotion

Anger is not only a complicated emotion, but a secondary one as well. It means that in most cases, anger is shown to mask another more primal emotion, like fear or sadness. Have you ever seen someone show anger and resentment after someone they love had left them? That is probably because they are trying to hide their pain behind the anger.

When two people in a relationship fight, angry comments flow between them in abundance. It's the fear of abandonment that usually makes them behave so. Sometimes, couples try to mask their vulnerability in the relationship by behaving in an angry manner, so that their partner cannot see the hurt inside them.

Similarly, people get angry after they've failed an exam, or been disqualified in a job interview. Behind this anger is a deep-seeded fear of the future, the feeling of letting down loved ones, and disappointments. Together, these deeper and more primal feelings surface as anger, making the real emotions almost invisible.

For most people, especially men, admitting to certain feelings is hard – fear, hopelessness, desperateness, and sometimes, love. This is the reason they hide their emotions behind anger, which is easier to show. This is one of the reasons that men are usually angrier than women in almost similar situations, because women are more comfortable in showing their real emotions.

Types of Anger

Did you know that there are actually several types of anger that we can experience? Some kinds of anger depends on the situation, the topic at hand that is aggravating us; other kinds of anger depend on our personalities, hence the terms "short-tempered", "cranky", "volatile", etc.

We can more or less distinguish a few types of anger – the people who always seem in a bad mood, forever angry; the types of people who tend to get angry suddenly, but recover very soon; the type of people who never show their rage but hold a grudge forever. These are the people we see around us everywhere, with their different levels of anger.

From a psychological perspective, however, anger is more complex than these regular types, and there can be diversification that we are not even aware of.

Volatile Anger

This kind of anger is more common in men than in women, especially if the men have a history of substance abuse. People with volatile anger can suddenly experience rage because of a simple reason, making us seem completely different from the person we are.

This anger makes us seem almost crazy in an instant. Seeing someone litter in the road, or someone giving us a push in a hurry – these incidents are enough for the person to become extremely angry in a second, to the point that we can start having seizures. More than just an emotion, volatile anger is actually considered a clinical condition known as Intermittent Explosive Disorder[1] People suffering from volatile anger are prone to violence or self-harm and need immediate consultation with a behavioral professional.

Passive-Aggressive Anger

Passive anger is suppressed anger; a person whose anger type is passive almost never expresses their true feelings. Instead of letting the world know they are angry, they use sarcastic and nasty remarks on the people around them, especially on the person they are angry with.

Passively angry people, beside sarcasm, show their anger in "sub-level" performance, or in trying to avoid the situation. When an employee is angry with their boss, they would express their anger by intentionally making mistakes in their work, or not completing their task. A partner in a relationship would show their anger by intentionally forgetting to do something their partner/spouse has asked them to do. They would, however, mask their purpose and plead ignorance or forgetfulness.

This kind of anger is hard to understand; the person who is angry is often mistaken as a rude or mean person. Even when extremely angry, they won't come clean about the reason for their anger, or ask for an apology or explanation. Their anger can be long-lasting, and they are also at risk of lashing out one day and becoming violent.

Chronic Anger

These people are always angry, and they prefer to stay that way. They go to bed angry and they wake up angry, and stay angry the whole day. There's nothing in particular that angers them; if they don't have anything to be mad about, they look for a reason to complain and criticize.

People with chronic anger can also make a record of their ability to hold on to anger. Months and years may pass, but they will still be angry over something trivial, referring to that topic whenever they can. Chronic anger is more of a habit than a reaction to an event, and if this goes on for years, the immune system suffers. Problems of the heart and hypertension are two problems common to a person with chronic anger.

Verbal Anger

Verbal anger is usually directed towards other people, and not at situations or circumstances. If for some reason, a person becomes angry with another, due to something that person has said or done, this kind of anger is formed.

Verbal anger is usually expressed in forms of words –

abusive, insulting, threatening words. This is not a very threatening form of anger; rather, the angry person actually feels better after they have expressed themselves verbally.

Overwhelming Anger

This kind of anger surfaces when a person becomes overwhelmed due to a situation, i.e. a looming deadline or the night before an important exam. Right before some overpowering event, the human mind sometimes fails to cope with the circumstances, leading to either frustration or helplessness. This is where the anger is born, because the individual can neither give up on the situation, nor advance towards it.

Mothers are prone to this kind of anger, especially when they feel overwhelmed with the responsibility of taking care of her young and demanding children. Overwhelming anger is a crucial part of post-partum depression – the feeling of wretchedness most new mother faces right after childbirth.

Moral/Judgmental or Empathetic Anger

These people think they have the right to show anger at any kind of injustice around them, even when they are not the direct victims. A random person breaking a simple rule on the road, i.e. honking when there's a hospital nearby, would make them extremely angry.

Usually, morally angry people are not a threat to anyone; they keep their anger within themselves simply by complaining about it or mumbling to themselves. However, they have a tendency to consider themselves superior to everyone else just because they had broken a few rules, and can show contempt and disrespect for others.

Addictive Anger

Some people are actually addicted to anger; they love the way anger makes them feel – full of adrenaline and rush of emotions. They actually go looking for reasons to get angry, and are more prone to get involved in a bar fight or disagreement in a stadium. Their anger is limited to a few insults and some punches, but otherwise not very harmful. What is remarkable is, however, people addicted to anger is out the next moment looking for another fight, not satisfied with the havoc they've created.

Self-Inflicted Anger

Anger at one's oneself is self-inflicted anger, possibly as punishment for doing something wrong or failing at something. This is a silent kind of anger, and the person suffering harms themselves – through self injury, starvation or refusing treatment for any illness.

Vengeful Anger

Sometimes, people become obsessed with someone who has wronged them in any way, and results in a very special kind of anger that demands revenge. This could be a minor injustice or a major one, but the victim, in their anger, starts to imagine themselves as a vigilante and plot revenge.

Most of the time, this kind of anger stays and dies within

the planning stage, but it is possible for the angry person to try their hand at actual revenge, especially if there's no one to stop them. If the fantasies of revenge are allowed to flourish, the end result could actually become violent or harmful; it is, therefore, better to keep a check on these revengeful thoughts at the first chance.

Petrified/Hardened Anger

When we are angry at someone, it is always better to show it and give the other person a chance to apologize or explain. If we don't receive at least a "sorry", that anger will keep on burning inside us and ultimately harden. It can go on for years and years and the person responsible won't even be aware of anything amiss.

Hardened anger is a very important reason behind many estrangements in relationships. Friendships have broken up and romantic involvements ended because of suppressed anger that has been increased inside year after year. The best way to deal with this kind of anger is to forgive the person we are angry with, and let bygones be bygones.

Incidental Anger

This is the most normal kind of anger there is, and a healthy one as well. Incidental anger is getting over a situation or an event, expressing it in a normal way, and then letting it go when the anger subsides. This is not only a healthy anger, but a necessary.

Incidental anger is proof that anger can be a good thing in our lives. How? You will find out in an upcoming chapter how anger is not all bad.

Paranoid Anger

Finally, paranoid anger – another very serious type of anger. People with paranoid anger suffer from the delusion that everyone around them is their enemy. They tend to view everyone as adversaries out to harm them. They suspect everyone and is often rude as well as angry.

The main reason behind their anger is their feeling of isolation as they have trouble trusting anyone, even their family members. They prefer to live a private life away from the people who, according to them, are "out to get them".

It is not necessary that a person has to fall in any one of these types of anger. Anger varies in people based on their personality, situation and attitude. Someone could have symptoms of more than one of these anger types, or something else entirely different.

More important than looking for a type is to understand what causes the anger in a person. These reasons, known as "triggers" of anger, could be anything - a specific topic, a person in particular, or an emotion. However, in most cases, it is a situation that makes people angry, circumstances they have trouble dealing with.

That's what we are going to discuss in the next segment of this book – triggers of anger.

What Triggers Anger?

What are the reasons that we get angry, suddenly and intensely? The answers are varied, and some of them might just surprise you.

Of course, anger varies in people. What might not bother someone at all can send another person screaming off the hill; the person who is always calm and understanding can suddenly get mad – that's how surprising this emotion is.

Feeling Helpless

Stranded in the rain without an umbrella or a transport, a flat tire on the highway, phone shutting down in the middle of an important call, being stuck in traffic before a meeting – these are all moments when we find ourselves helpless to do anything. These are everyday problems that we more or less face in our lives, and different people react to them in their own manner. We might become sad or annoyed at our helplessness, but mostly, these are situations where people show anger.

Injustice

Injustice is also something that is common in our lives, in big and small forms. Not getting the promotion we deserve, getting robbed or hijacked, being the victim of a crime, being shouted at by a teacher or our boss – the viciousness of injustice falls on us all. What do we do when something like this happens to us? Our initial reaction is, usually, to get angry.

Ridicule or Insult

It is easy to understand why people might get angry at being ridiculed or when insulted. How would you feel if someone insults you, calls you names, makes fun of you or ridicules you in front of others? Of course, your first instinct would be to get very, very angry. If you are young or hotheaded, you might even get angry enough to lurch at the person insulting you, hurting them physically. This is why anger is always elevated in a quarrel, because almost no one in this world can stay normal when they are being ridiculed or insulted.

Disrespect

Disrespectful attitude and behavior always triggers anger in people – impudence, being lied to, being cheated, not paid attention or not listened to, direct disregard of our wishes, and many more. In the old days, showing disrespect to someone else would have taken the matter down to duels. Since that is not possible in the modern times, the usual reaction happens to be anger.

Failure

Whether we've come second in a race or done badly in a test – anger follows. It is the feeling of failure in a person that makes us angry when we are unsuccessful in something, even if it is a very trivial matter. Most people are competitive in nature, and failing in something naturally causes anger in us. It is, however, a trait found more in adults. Have you ever seen a toddler getting angry because it has fallen down when learning to walk?

Feeling Let Down

It is women who are more likely to feel angry when they feel let down by someone close to them. Women, in general, expect more from their loved ones – partners, parents, children and friends – and they are more hurt when they feel used or unappreciated. Behind this kind of anger is a wound, which emerges when they are unable to find the right balance in their relationships.

Frustration

Frustration is the feeling you get when something or someone is blocking you on your way to your goal. Unable to follow up on your vacation plans because of work? Impossible to go out because of rain? Unable to buy the latest iPhone because you don't have the money? What you will be feeling is frustration, which could easily trigger anger in a person.

Hunger

There's actually a special term for this – Hangry. We don't usually understand or pay attention to this particular feeling, but hunger can actually make a normal situation much, much worse by making us angry. There are some days in all of our lives when we feel extremely angry and frustrated and not realize the reason behind it. In truth, it is the lack of food in our stomach which makes us cranky and irritated.

Violation of Privacy

None of us like to be asked too many questions, especially questions about our private life. Unfortunately nosy people are everywhere, people who don't understand the word 'privacy' or 'personal space'. This is the reason celebrities get angry when the paparazzi follow them everywhere, because their privacy is violated. If we have such a person in our lives – a nosy neighbor or an overbearing friend – who is always poking into our lives, it is normal to be angry.

Disturbances and Disruptions

There's always that one person on the road who is going to blare their horns even when there's no way to go, that person who will definitely try to cut in a queue, the type of people whose phone won't be off in a theater. These are all reasons for others to experience anger, and I don't blame you when that happens. These kind of disturbances and disruptions – like the person who is definitely going to interrupt you a thousand times in the middle of a story – are absolutely reasons to get angry.

Pain or Suffering

People who are ill or bed-ridden are usually cranky; they tend to get angry very easily, at the slightest provocation. That's what illness and suffering does to a person, it makes a person angry. If you or someone else close to you is ill or in pain, it will be normal for them to be mad almost all the time.

Apart from these obvious reasons which make almost everyone angry, there are some other vague reasons, such as:

- If you are unhappy in a relationship
- If you are extremely tired with no chance of rest any time soon
- If you are sexually frustrated
- If someone has used abusive language with you

- If you are feeling controlled by someone else
- If you are having financial trouble
- If you are being judged by someone
- If you are under a lot of stress at work or at home
- If someone is shaming you
- If you have been physically threatened
- If you are feeling unloved by someone special
- If you are being ignored by your peers

Besides, there can be instances when you are simply aggravated by looking at someone. This is quite normal, too, for a person to be so annoyed with someone else without any reason. This usually happens with a malicious colleague or a snooping relative – people you have to interact with even when you don't want to.

So, it has been established that we face a number of situations to get angry every day, causing us to show our temper. But do you know how to recognize anger, in yourself or in someone else in the room?

How to Recognize Anger?

Well, someone screaming *"I'm angry! I have never been so angry in my life before!"* could be the perfect sign of anger. So would thrashing around and screaming – but that's not what everyone does.

In many cases, the signs of anger are subtle; it is very difficult to understand that a person is actually angry before it's too late to calm them down. Besides, if we are dealing with someone else's anger issues, it is important that we know what they are capable of behaving like in extreme anger.

How to recognize anger, in ourselves and in others – that's what this part of the book is concerned with!

Signs of an Angry Person

Anger may be an emotion, but it is very much visible from the outside, unlike many other feelings we experience throughout the day. Most of the signs of an angry person can be of two several types.

The physical indications of anger may include:

- Excessive sweating, more than is normal
- Sweating palms and sole of the feet
- Excessive shaking and trembling
- Heart beating fast
- Experiencing headaches
- Feeling warm around the neck and face
- Clenching fists
- Unknowingly grinding teeth together
- Feeling dizzy and lightheaded
- Feeling slight or acute pain in the stomach

Mentally and emotionally, you will also go through a number of feelings, including:

- Irritated by everyone around you, even if there are no reasons

- Not having the patience to deal with the situation
- Feelings of sadness hanging over yourself
- Anxious for the phase to pass
- Feeling blank when you try to express your feelings
- Guilty for the situation you have created
- Resentful of everyone who is trying to help you

Your behavior will change too, making you:

- Raise your voice when speaking
- More sarcastic than you usually are
- Craving some cigarettes, or a drink, or anything you are addicted to
- Lose any sign of sense of humor
- Completely unsympathetic to anyone
- Blame others for your feelings, even if the fault was yours
- Call everyone insulting names
- Pace around as if you are anxious
- Criticize and belittle everyone
- Want to leave the situation immediately to get away from everything
- Start crying
- Shut down
- Argue with everyone without any apparent reason
- Scream at others

Apart from these signs that almost everyone shows

when angry, there are a couple of other symptoms that should be taken as warning. When in excessive anger, if a person starts showing these signs, it might mean they can get violent or abusive.

Warning signs of anger can be the following:

- Breathing fast, as if the person is having trouble
- Stare at other people in a threatening or aggressive manner
- Throwing things that are close at hand
- Punching at walls
- Screaming very loudly, but not saying anything
- Pacing up and down very fast
- Cupping a fist with another hand
- Rubbing or pressing the head as if in pain
- Rocking the body to and fro in a rhythm
- Raising a hand as if to hit someone

If these warning signs become frequent and extreme, it is indeed time to seek some help in anger management therapy before something regretful happens.

How can Anger harm us?

Anger may be an emotion, but its affect goes beyond just the usual harm on our mental self. Rather, anger may be the most destructive emotion there is in the human world, with the ability to harm our health, our relationships, our careers, our social life as well as our mental peace.

Most of the effects of anger are destructive, negative and

extremely powerful. The bouts of anger may be over in a matter of minutes, but its effect is long-lasting and sometimes, fatal.

Effect on Our Body

Ever heard of the 'flight or fight' response? That's what happens to our body when we get angry – our body prepares itself to either fight what's bothering us, or take a flight. Either way, the body goes through a number of changes, the same way it does when we experience fear or too much excitement.

In the 'flight or fight response', the body is flooded with adrenaline and cortisol – two stress hormones from the adrenaline gland. These are the hormones that are responsible for the way our body reacts to fear and physical threat, by giving us almost superhuman strength to deal with the problem at hand.

Besides, the blood gathers in our muscles, in case we need to exert physical force – as is possible in case of imminent danger. All this extra energy and special hormones make us strong enough to tackle any opponent, leading us to violence.

Effect on the Heart

The heart is not spared in this emotion; rather, it plays a central role. The blood vessels in our body tighten up when we are angry; blood pressure sky-rockets. The body becomes energized and ready for action which, if not controlled, can lead to heart attacks.

According to Dr. Chris Aiken, who is the Director of the Mood Treatment Center[2] in North Carolina, the risk of having a heart attack doubles in the hours following an angry outburst. In his study[3] on this topic, he found that people who are frequently angry have twice the chance of suffering from heart diseases and heart attacks than people who are rarely angry.

Effect on the Brain

An angry outburst doesn't only increase the chances of a heart stroke, but the risk of a stroke as well. Explained in a paper titled "Outburst of anger as a trigger of acute cardiovascular events"[4] by Dr. E Mostofsky, Dr. E.A. Penner and Dr. M.A. Mittleman in 2014, the study states that the risk of a clot in the brain increases 3 times in a person after an outburst. If the person in question has an aneurism in their brain, the risk increases 6 times!

Effect on the Immune System

If you are the type of person who is often angry, it's safe to assume that your immune system isn't up to the mark. We may not be aware of it, but there is a direct link between staying sick almost all the time and too much suppressed anger in a person.

Here's your proof - a scientific paper published in 2016 by Dr. A. Romero-Martinez, Dr. M. Lila, Dr. S. Vitoria-Estruch and Dr. L. Moya-Alboil titled "High

Immunoglobulin A Levels Mediate the Association Between High Anger Expression and Low Somatic Symptoms in Intimate Partner Violence Perpetrators"[5]. According to this study, a bout of anger in an otherwise healthy person causes a reduction in the Antibody Immunoglobulin, which is the main cell in the human body that defends any kinds of infection. The more prone we are to anger, the more our immunity system deteriorates, leaving us defenseless against diseases.

Effect on Longevity of Life

It is indeed true that happy and content people live longer, especially because there isn't much place for anxiety and anger in their lives. On the other hand, anger leads to stress, and a life filled with unnecessary stress is neither a happy nor a long one.

Effect on Your Lungs

Another surprising effect of anger – on your lungs! The health of your lungs don't only depend on the fact whether you are a smoker or not, but whether you are often angry. Especially in older males, frequent anger attacks and a hostile attitude can worsen the capacity of the lungs, and even result in asthma.

According to a paper published in 2008 titled "Angry breathing: A prospective study of hostility and lung function in the Normative Aging Study"[6], anger can actually inflame our airways and create problem in breathing. This study was conducted by Dr. L. D. Kubzansky, Dr. D. Sparrow, Dr. B.

Jackson, Dr. S. Cohen, Dr. S. T. Weiss, and Dr. R. J. Wright from USA.

Effect on Our Mental Health

Since this is an emotion we are dealing, it is logical that excessive and regular anger will be harmful for our peace of mind.

Anger and Depression

Not everybody vents and lashes out in their anger; some people prefer to suppress it within themselves. This kind of repressed anger, known as passive anger, has been linked by scientists to depression.

When we can't express how angry we are but try to hide it inside us, it can emerge as depression. Anger and depression are very closely related in the human mind, together with pain. Even if the depression isn't directly caused by the anger, suppressed rage fuels depressed thoughts to a great extent, making people withdraw more and more into themselves.

Anger and Sleep

Ever tried to sleep while you are still angry? It's almost impossible to fall asleep when you are seething and restless, let alone have a good night's sleep. What happens next when you spend a sleepless night tossing and turning? You go through the day feeling cranky and moody, murderous even.

This is indeed a vicious cycle that goes on and on. Sleep

deprivation is common in the life of an angry person, and its effect on our health is excruciating. Anxiety increases, so does the chance of obesity and weight gain, stress more than doubles because of sleep deprivation; not only that, risk of heart attacks and hypertension also increases. To be concise, life generally becomes miserable because of too much anger keeping up alive at nights.

Anger and Anxiety

If you are constantly angry, it is possible that you are also a world class worrier. Indeed, anger and anxiety are always present together in a person. All the signs of suppressed anger, i.e. hostility towards a person, sarcastic and mean remarks, aggressive behavior – these all contribute towards anxiety.

Suppressed anger is one of the biggest reasons behind Generalized Anxiety Disorder (GAD)[7], which is the immense worry that people with this disorder live with every single day of their lives. GAD is a serious problem in a big percentage of the population and often requires clinical help; anger is a huge part of that problem.

Anger and Guilt

Usually, bouts of anger are followed by an immense sense of guilt. The person who has just created a scene only moments ago goes through a variety of emotions – embarrassment, remorse, self-loathing, shame, to the extent of self-loathing. They hate themselves for insulting and hurting people they love and in their remorse, often think of self-injury or suicide.

These feelings are not good for our mental peace; rather, feeling like this continuously can seriously trouble the mind and make a person do something drastic.

Effect on Relationships

No one wants to live with an angry person. Justified and irregular outbreaks of anger in a person can be dealt with, but not when they become frequent and regular. Who would want to be with someone who is always throwing tantrums over simple events, or being sarcastic and rude to everyone? *No one!*

It is marriages and romantic involvements that suffer the most because of anger. In these relationships, two people can become as close as is possible for any human being, letting them know all about each other. If one person in the relationship is always getting angry and exploding on the other one, there is a limit to how much the other person can suffer. Life can become very uncomfortable for two people to live together in a closed space when one of them has the tendency to get angry at the slightest provocation.

In most cases, people are scared of partners with an angry streak; there is every reason to fear an outburst at any moment – social outings, family functions, in public or in private moments. It is also not uncommon for someone to avoid their partner as much as they can, which may not always be possible.

Suppressed anger in a relationship will ultimately destroy it, causing breakups and divorces. When issues are not solved and a lot is left unsaid, the bitterness under the relationship gradually increases, leaving the partners no choice but to separate, leading to pain and heartbreaks. These kinds of problems in relationships are especially hard if there are children involved, which makes the matter much more complicated.

Effect on Children

As I said before, anger is especially hard on children in a family, when they have to grow up with a parent who is always outraged. Add alcohol or substance abuse to the equation and the children from such a family will have a wretched childhood, guaranteed!

A parent's job is hard, and it is very normal for a father or a mother to get angry every now and then. But when a child has to live with a parent who is constantly angry with them, criticizes and insults them at every opportunity, the child becomes fearful of the people who are supposed to be the closest to them in the world.

Children living with angry parent(s) become more and more aggressive as they grow up; if they had seen their parents being violent and abusive, that's the attitude they assume in life as well. Male children grow up to abuse their partners, and the female children choose an abusive partner and silently endure mistreatment – that's the tendency everywhere.

When the parents are constantly angry and abusive, children grow up with low-self esteem; they live in fear and anxiety, and ultimately become angry themselves. In many cases, alcohol and substance becomes a part of their lives, as a mean to escape from reality.

Children do not have the coping skills needed to handle anger as adults do; neither do they have the ability to leave the person who is frightening them. It is much harder for them to grow up with a vicious person in their lives, and it affects them much more than it would a grown-up.

Effect on Other People

It's not just our partners and children who are affected by our frequent angry outbursts, but almost everyone around us. Just like your positive attitudes can influence your social circle – parents, siblings, friends and relatives, your angry attitude can also make them apprehensive and weary.

If you are prone to sudden and random outbursts of anger, it's a guarantee you won't be welcome anywhere. Your presence will make everyone nervous and fearful, and even the people closest to you will tiptoe around you. No one is ever really comfortable with someone who can flare up any moment and create a scene in a social gathering. If you get fewer and fewer invitations to parties and get-togethers, the reason could be your uncontrollable anger. After all, you can't expect other people to put up with your anger issues forever!

Even your parents, the people who are supposed to love you unconditionally, have trouble getting past the anger issues of their offspring. Most of the people who have problem controlling their anger, unfortunately, unleash the wrath on people who are the closest, which includes parents. Anger is a big reason that parents feel alienated from their children, because they can't understand the reasons no matter how much they try to help.

Effect on Your Career

When other people in your life have trouble putting up with your issues, why wouldn't the people you work with? Your boss and your colleagues aren't even related to you, neither are they responsible for your well-being.

Your sudden outbursts of anger won't be welcome in the workplace, even if you are the owner or the CEO. Your colleagues and your employees deserve to be respected and valued, not to be screamed at. While hostility and jealousy is normal at the workplace, a big outrage can de-motivate the others and actually decrease productivity.

Passive aggressive anger is also very common at the workplace. In this kind of anger, a person doesn't show their anger but suppress it – as I've discussed earlier. Instead of screaming or yelling, they start making sarcastic remarks; they might even intentionally under-perform in order to punish their boss. Ultimately, it is the angry person who is in the losing side, because someone who underperforms and is mean to other people in the workplace will not go very far.

If you are the owner or the CEO of a company and have anger issue, can you hope to take your organization far? In a nutshell, you will have trouble with all your clients, suppliers, competitors as well as employees – leaving your organization to suffer the consequences.

Effect during Pregnancy

Pregnancy could be a wonderful experience for parents-to-be, or a hard one; there's no question that this is one of the most important phases of a person's life. Although it is the woman who bears the child, the responsibility is on both parents. If one of them, or both, has anger issues, it can harm the unborn child.

The mother goes through a number of changes during pregnancy - some of them nice, but mostly uncomfortable. It is the excess presence of hormones in her body that can make the mother feel frustrated, sad or angry. If the anger reaches a dangerous point, the changes in the body – namely, rise in blood pressure and heart rate – can be distressful to the child.

Again, if the father - or the other partner – is the one with anger issues, it will create anxiety and stress in the mother. Stress is probably the worst thing that can happen to an expectant mother; too much worrying and tension is the leading cause of miscarriages in pregnancy, according to trusted sources[8].

Effect on Our Spirit

Not the type of anger that suddenly flares up and then quickly dies, but the type of anger that people holds on to - those are what effects not only physically and mentally, but also spiritually.

The effect of short-lived anger is not so harmful on our spirit; but when a person spends years seething in anger, their spirit becomes bitter and acidic. A bitter spirit opens the door to other evils - hatred, jealousy and pride to name a few. The heart that is full of anger is not a positive heart, but a pessimist one; an angry spirit cannot see the beauty of the world, will feel far from God, and neither can it appreciate all the good things in life.

It is a sad world waiting for people who are always angry, constantly holding a grudge against others. Their spirit is greatly harmed, and they will not be able to enjoy all the happiness that only a happy spirit can.

Effect on Society

Most of the criminals and lawbreakers of our society act in anger. It seems like everywhere we look, someone with anger in their hearts and a gun in their hands is creating havoc – murdering a group of innocent people.

Sometimes it is sudden anger over their personal problems that make them blind for the moment, leading them to commit crimes they were not planning to. At other times, suppressed anger ultimately reaches its pinnacle one day, causing the person to snap. In many other cases, crimes of anger are actually someone taking revenge because they are mad at a person.

In the United States of America, there have been 207 cases of school shootings since 2003. In 1999, two students - Eric and Dylan- shot and killed 11 of their classmates and 1 teacher, and injured 23 others[9].Both boys were angry over being bullied at school and had developed a personality disorder which reached its pinnacle on that fateful day. After killing off all the people who had bullied and tortured them at school, they committed suicide inside the school library. *(Source:* http://news.jrn.msu.edu*).*

From 2001 to 2012, more than 11,766 women have been killed in USA by their husbands or partners, according to an astonishing report by FBI. Most of these crimes have been in anger – the male partner suspecting the women of cheating or killing them in sudden rage. The number of women who are regularly beaten and abused by angry partners are much higher than this number. *(Source: http://www.upworthy.com).*

In 2013, 35-year-old Ceri Fuller murdered his three children (12, 8 and 7 years old) after a fight with his wife. When 34-year old Ruth Fuller admitted to have feelings for another man, her husband - in extreme anger - killed their sleeping children and committed suicide, only to punish his wife for her betrayal. *(Source:* http://www.dailymail.co.uk*)*[10].

If we take a look behind all the crimes committed in the world, anger would be lurking somewhere in the background. Indeed, this is a very powerful emotion that can completely change a person in a matter or moments, making them unrecognizable.

However, anger can be good too, did you know?

Is Anger Always Bad?

After reading about so many harmful effect of anger, it is normal that this question comes to the mind – "Is anger always bad?" The answer is 'no'. Anger isn't always bad; rather, in some situations, it could actually be a good thing.

It is true that excessive anger too often in our lives is certainly not something desirable, but there are some times during our days when a little display of anger can actually be helpful. In this part of the book, let's see how anger can actually be helpful sometimes.

Anger can be Motivational

When we fail at something, there can be two different ways to feel about it – either we can be dejected and sad, or we can become angry. If we are sad, it is unlikely that we can find it in ourselves to stand up and try again. We will probably be too busy feeling sad for ourselves and let the matter go.

However, if our initial reaction is anger, what will come to our mind are thoughts like:

> *–This is not supposed to happen to me!*
> *–I am not ready to admit defeat!*
> *–This is not the end of me!*
> *–I refuse to be beaten!*

Only anger can trigger reactions like this, which is way better than getting discouraged and giving up. There are thousands of motivational stories around us where people have used their anger to rise from the ashes and try again. Indeed, anger and the feeling of decision that follows it, could be a great motivation in times of need.

Anger can be Insightful

In many cases, bouts of anger are followed by a sense of realization. What a suffering mind cannot realize can become clear to a person who had just had an outburst.

It is when we are angry that we can finally release everything we had been suppressing in ourselves – aggravation, pain, complaints, accusations and sufferings. The mind becomes clear. It becomes easier to look inside ourselves, to find out our faults instead of just blaming others. Besides, after an angry outburst, it is possible for the person in question to feel guilty, learn what's really important in their life.

Anger can be the Push you need

It is often that we cannot act correctly in the face of injustice. Someone pushing and shoving in a queue, being unfairly blamed for something, someone else getting the promotion we deserve – these kinds of injustice usually go unprotected. Anger is the perfect push we need to protest these unfair situations of our life.

Getting angry is sometimes the best reaction we can

have to an occurrence, especially if we've just experienced unfairness. Without getting angry, we might not be able to protest back, to demand what is rightfully ours, or to dispute if we are in the wrong.

Anger can Protect

Imagine there's someone threatening to hurt your child, or someone else you love. In such monumental situations, your anger will push you ahead. In anger mode, your body will initiate the "fight or flight" approach, helping you with the courage to take action. Otherwise, fear and hesitation might make you feel weak, and unable to do anything.

In times of need, it is anger that will help you the most, more than any other emotions. You need an emotion as strong as anger to help you through and to give you courage.

Anger can be Productive

Over the years, there had been many instances when anger had played a significant role in many important social causes. When slavery was abolished in the United States of America or when women were given the right to vote, anger was present behind all the political bureaucracy and law.

The Mothers Against Drunk Driving (MADD)[11] association was formed in 1980 by a group of angry mothers who have lost their loved ones in accidents caused by drunk drivers. Similarly, People for the Ethical Treatment of Anumals (PETA)[12] is an organization with more than 5 million supporters united against cruelty on animals. These two ideas are the perfect example how responsible people have used their anger against drunk drivers and torturers of animals for constructive causes.

Anger can be Preventive

It is entirely possible than suppressing anger can ultimately lead to self-destructive ideas, like harming or hurting ourselves. People who show the tendency to hide their feelings are more likely to attempt suicide or harm themselves. Hiding anger for a long time can result in an implosion, creating more problems than before. On the other hand, the type of people who are prone to outbursts can control themselves better.

In the same way, if we explode one day after hiding years of resentment inside us, the result can be violent. Regular outbursts of anger can be harmful but not really destructive; it is suppressed anger that actually makes us violent enough to physically harm someone, even someone we love.

Anger can be Healing

Angry outbursts can actually be healthy at time; at least, showing anger is much better than restraining our emotions. Anger makes us open up and speak our mind which, ultimately, is healing for our health as well as for our mental peace.

Anger can get the Work Done

When you've tried being nice and failed to make someone listen – a child or an employee – the next best thing would be to show some anger. Sometimes, cajoling, bribing or requesting won't work, but an angry outburst just might.

> *–Children not picking up their toys after playtime, no matter how many times you talk to them? Try getting angry at them!*
>
> *–Employee failing to come to work on time, even after multiple warnings? Try anger!*
>
> *–Neighbors listening to music loudly after you've complained many times? Get angry and give them a visit!*

Yes, sometimes you definitely need the help of anger to get the work done, especially after being civil hasn't helped.

But most importantly, showing your anger – not always, but every now and then – can actually be good for you. When you are feeling angry over something, why not let it show? Just keep in mind that – it doesn't get so bad that you end up saying or doing something you will regret later.

Part Two: Managing Your Anger

In most of the cases, just a little precaution on your part can save you a lot of trouble later. Checking yourself before your anger gets a hold of you, or recognizing your personal triggers, or even just removing yourself from the scene - that's how little it takes to avoid an angry outburst.

Managing your anger is indeed possible, and can actually be easy, if you know the steps. All you need is a little alertness, looking into yourself for a few minutes, and you can conquer this dangerous enemy.

Just as it is hard living with sudden and uncontrollable anger, it is harder living with someone who has anger issues. That can be overcome too, with the right techniques - all of which has been discussed in this portion of the book.

So, happy reading, and hope this helps you!

Don't Give in to Anger

Prevention is better than cure, right?

Right! So, before you want to learn how to stop overreacting in anger or how to apologize to everyone you've insulted and hurt in the process, you need to try and stop anger in its tracks.

Yes, it may be hard, but it is definitely possible.

Prevention #1: Identify the Reason

You're at work, dealing with an urgent project with a looming deadline, and you suddenly find yourself getting angry. You feel this uncontrollable rage building up inside you and you realize that any moment now, you might start screaming and possibly throw away your files in frustration.

Stop right there, and take a long breath; then, ask yourself: *what am I angry about?* At a first glance, it may seem like you are frustrated about your work progressing slow and worried about the deadline that is creeping up on you.

However the reason could be something deeper than that, another issue which may not be important to you at that moment. It might be:

> *—that you have not been performing your best at work recently and worried about your job;*
> *—that you don't really like your job and your workplace makes you feel suffocated;*

—that no matter how much you work, your boss takes all the credit;

—that you've been having some problems with your spouse/partner and don't know how to handle it;

—that a loved one is sick at home;

—that you've had a restless night and very little sleep;

—that you didn't have the time for breakfast in the morning and feeling hungry;

—that you desperately need a vacation, SOON!

Couples fight all the time, but some fights can accelerate into something bigger and much more damaging. Imagine a silly fight about the TV remote turning into talks about divorce and leaving each other. Yes, that can happen when couples get serious in a fight - fighting over the silliest of topics can end in someone saying *"I want a divorce!"* What are you really fighting about - what show to watch? That could certainly seem to be the reason, but chances are that it can be something even more profound - an issue you haven't even thought about for years.

- Maybe you feel like you never get your way around your partner;

- Maybe you have the kind of personality that everyone takes advantage of;

- Maybe you've always hated this particular habit of your partner;

- Maybe you feel as if your partner doesn't treat you with proper respect;

- Maybe you are just exhausted of other people always getting what they want;

- Maybe you have been recently having doubts about your relationship.

See? The fight about the TV remote could have just been the tip of the iceberg; the problem behind the fight could have been something much, much deeper.

As I've said before, anger is a complex emotion; anger is often used to hide some other more primal in people. Disappointment, fear of abandonment, sense of failure, worry about the future, afraid that you are not being a good provider for your family - these deeper emotions are hidden behind an angry outburst.

That's the best step you can take to control your anger *before* it gets out of hand. There's no guarantee that looking for the actual problem behind your anger will help you overcome it or never to get angry again. What thinking about the reason will do is that, they might surprise you at the moment! The real reason why you are angry and the apparent reason you thought was bothering you could be very, very different from each other. Surprise, surprise!

So the next time you find yourself getting angry, stop to take a moment before you express your anger. Ask yourself this simple question: *why exactly am I getting angry? Is it because of the looming deadline/I really want to watch my favorite show, or something entirely different?*

By luck, this question will keep you distracted for a few moments while your anger diffuses!

Prevention #2: Avoid your Triggers

We all have some particular anger triggers that makes us lose our temper. I have provided a detailed list of all the triggers common to people in the previous part of this book. Some of them might seem familiar to you after you have spend some time thinking about them.

Some anger triggers are easy to recognize and deal with before an angry outburst. *Example: hunger.* The moment you realize your anger could be due to the fact that you are hungry, a big portion of something, will definitely calm you down. I mean, try giving an extremely cranky person a greasy, gooey burger filled with meat and mayonnaise, and a can of Coca-Cola; it won't take them more than a second to calm down at the sight of it!

Some more complex triggers are, unfortunately, harder to deal with, namely - frustration, feeling let down, helplessness or disrespect. But still there's a way! If you can't directly deal with these triggers, the next best thing would be to avoid them!

There! Avoid your triggers as much as you can, and they won't have the power to upset or enrage you.

Here are some ingenious tips for the question, *"But how?"*

See someone who makes you angry, without any apparent reason? We've all got someone like that in our lives. The moment you see this person or they open their mouth, you feel like putting your fists through a car windshield? So, avoid this person; literally cross the road if you see them on your side. Fish out your phone and keep your eyes glued to the screen, behave as if you haven't seen them. I don't recommend this WHILE you are crossing the road, obviously!

If you are unlucky, that person could be someone unavoidable, i.e. a colleague, a relative, a neighbor, friend of a spouse or spouse of a friend, or your in-laws. You can't really avoid or ignore these people and not become a social pariah.

If that's the case, limit your interactions to the minimum "Hello", "Lovely weather" and "Goodbye!" Excuse yourself and leave as soon as possible. If they go on talking, let your mind go "La La La!" or watch the sky. Better yet, think about your next vacation; that will give you the strength to bear with this unfortunate turn of event.

Morale of the story: don't give them the chance to get you angry!

People who have recently given up smoking get angry when they see other people around them enjoying a smoke.

If this is your trigger, you need to avoid places where people are allowed to smoke - certain restaurants and bars, preferably. If you are with people who smoke, explain the situation to them and hope they understand. If they are not sympathetic, and thus falling into the category of people you can't tolerate, make and excuse and leave.

You might be a laid-back person who enjoys their 'not doing anything' time, but hate it when people call you lazy or idle. You know inside that you are not lazy, but that you prefer to spend your life the way you want to, and people insulting you by calling you sluggish makes you mad.

The solution is simple: avoid those people. Whenever the topic arises, change the direction of the conversation. This could be important at family events when a distant relative you don't even like takes it on themselves to comment on your lifestyle. Instead of getting mad, change the topic and talk about something else. If you are not successful in this, make an excuse and leave.

Injustices make us angry, particularly if we can't do anything about. But in many cases, it is actually possible to make a difference - albeit a small one - if we are just brave enough to take a stand. It's better to stand up and protest when someone cuts in before you in a queue or takes your parking space. Instead of getting angry inside, tell that person what they are doing is wrong and to apologize. When you are the first person to make a stand, others will follow and you will get your justice. Even if you don't, the satisfaction of 'actually doing something' will be enough for you to not get angry.

If you are angry about some bigger injustices in life - i.e. war, people starving in poor countries, natural disasters that you can't do anything to stop - do your best to help. Join in a protest or gather resources to send over, volunteer in good causes so that you have the satisfaction of helping. You can do much good in helping and protesting for a day than by sulking over an issue for a whole year!

Noisy upstairs neighbors making you mad with their daily practice of... tap dancing? If the sound is bothering you too much, try to stay out of the house every day. If this is not the time to stay out, talk to your neighbors so that they change the timing of their practice to the hours you are not home.

If they are nice people, they'll understand. If they disregard your request, you have the choice: either stay out when they are practicing, use ear plugs, or buy a loud guitar to play at the stroke of midnight!

Facing traffic every day when you come back from work? The solution could be easy if you have the chance. Shift the time you get out of the office to an hour later so that you completely miss the rush hour. An hour after everyone has rushed out of their offices to go home, you can find the traffic relatively lighter.

If you are not willing to work the extra hour, you don't need to. Find a quite little café around your workplace and grab a drink. Enjoy your drink in peace, probably with a good book, while the rest of the world rushes outside. There's one hour you have to yourself, with no one to bother you, doing exactly what you want to with your time. By the time the hour is up, you will feel energized after a long day at work, and ready to go home to your family.

Nosy neighbor or relative asking very personal questions or that doesn't respect boundaries? Instead of getting angry, just be honest with them. Say something like, "I can't think of any reason why I should share this information with you!" Sometimes, you need to be clear if you want someone to back off and leave you alone.

As children, we all had this ingenious game of imitating grown-ups, remember? Whatever they said, we'd say the exact same thing and watch them go berserk! There's no need to assume that we can't still play that game because we're the grown-ups.

The next time someone says something insulting or provocative, reply with a shrug and a "To each his own, man!" or a "You'd know that, wouldn't you?" Fun, right? Other such answers are "Right back at you, mate!" and "Mind if I ignore you some other time?" These aren't direct insults so you are not really being rude; these are rather imaginative ways for you to momentarily disarm your opinion without losing temper.

The feeling of helplessness can sometimes trigger anger; but if you are a little prepared, you can avoid many such circumstances. As with the examples above in the part about feeling helpless; carrying an umbrella will save you from the rain, a phone charger or a portable battery charger will help you keep your phone alive, and a knowledge of tires and an extra tire will help avoid such situations.

All you need is to be a little alert, and you can avoid many such helpless situations which might have made you lose your anger!

Granted, there are some triggers in life that you can't ignore; but there are also a lot of situations that you *can* handle very easily without losing your temper and creating a scene. The best prevention can be to avoid these situations altogether, ignore the people who aggravate you and think - really think - about what's troubling you.

No, you are not taking the coward's way out by escaping these situations. Look at it this way: *you are trying your best to avoid a bad situation.* You are taking the high way and avoiding direct confrontation, so that you don't lose your temper and do something that you might regret later.

Controlling Sudden Anger

No matter how much you try, sometimes, there's just no escaping anger. Thinking won't help; neither will trying to avoid your triggers. Some tempers are so sudden and powerful, you'll have to bear through them.

No, I am not going to give you fruitless suggestions like "try and keep calm" and "relax yourself" because that doesn't work, not when you are fuming mad. It's easy to advice others to "let it go" and "be the bigger person" but these advices doesn't sound good when you are on the receiving end.

What I am actually going to discuss in this chapter are some practical and effective - but also easy - tricks to help you control yourself when you face the possibility of an angry outburst.

Trick #1: The Classic Countdown Trick

It may be the oldest trick in the book, but it really works, especially if you are looking forward to calming your mind. This technique also helps if you are feeling restless, agitated or frustrated.

The steps are simple really. On the onset of an angry outburst, start counting backwards: 10 ... 9 ... 8 ... 7 ... 6 ... 5 ... 4 ... 3 ... 2 ... 1. That's 10 seconds to shift your focus away from what's happening around to aggravate you. If possible, close your eyes and do the counting; this way, you are also blocking the view of the situation or person making you angry. Remove yourself from the situation, mentally if not physically.

If it doesn't work, do it again - a little slower, if you can. Take 30 seconds to count from 10 to 1, taking a breath between each number. Do it from 50 if you are excessively angry: 50...49...48...47...46...45...and so on. By the time you have reached around 25, your mind will definitely feel calmer and chances are, you will half forget what you were angry about before.

Trick #2: Try a Breathing Exercise

Now this trick will only work if you can remove yourself from the situation aggravating you and take a few moments for yourself. Otherwise, if you close your eyes and start breathing heavily in front of someone, they will come to the conclusion that you are probably ill and call an ambulance!

So, the next time you feel a bout of anger coming in - i.e. your boss is screaming at you, or your children throwing a tantrum, remove yourself from the site. Get into a restroom or any other empty room, or back to your seat; sit down and close your eyes. Now, breathe!

Take long breaths, and focus on your breaths as they go in and out of your lungs. Try to feel the air when you breathe it in, feel in travelling through your nostrils and filling your lungs. Take a moment while the air is fresh in your lungs, then slowly and gently, breathe out. While exhaling, follow the same routine and carefully observe the whole process.

Something as simple and automatic as breathing should consume your whole concentration so that you are not thinking of anything else for those few minutes. Continue this breathing exercise for a few times - at least 12 or 13 times until you can feel your mind clearing and your temper cooling down. The best place for this exercise would be outside, somewhere with a lot of trees and fresh air; if that's not possible, inside the room is fine.

Normally when we breathe, we take in short gulps of air just enough to survive. The amount of air we inhale doesn't fill our lungs the way it's supposed to; the respiratory system doesn't get to work to its full capacity. This is why, when we actually concentrate on our breathing and take in a lungful of air - we immediately start to feel better. This way, we are breathing the way we are supposed to breathe. Our brain also receives better and more oxygen and becomes fresher, working better.

Moreover, we are shifting our focus to one single activity, giving our mind the time to cool down and assess the situation, instead of reacting. This is a great way to deal with sudden and overwhelming anger - diverting our mind to concentrate on something else.

Trick #3: Shift Your Concentration

I imagine this has happened to almost everyone out there: you are driving through the traffic and there's a car behind/beside you who is constantly honking for no apparent reason. Neither can you move and give the car space, nor can you block out the sound; seems like this driver is honking loudly just for the sake of it, and you can't do anything about it because you are just as stuck in the traffic as s/he is.

Now, the normal reaction to this situation would be to get angry, get out of the car, go up to the other car and start screaming. You might also feel like dragging the driver out of the car and start punching. Well, that's hardly possible - seeing that we live in a society that frowns upon such acts!

What you can do is to shift your focus away from the honking driver and look somewhere else. The sky, for instance, or the bumper sticker on the car in front of you, the kids playing in the next car, street signs, your own reflection in the mirror - anything at all but not at the car behind irritating you. Turn on the radio and pay extra attention to the music playing; hum to the song or try to learn the lyrics. Don't just think of something else, just find anything other than that car to actually look at and concentrate on. You can absolutely look at anything except what's bothering you.

The same trick also comes in handy while you are standing in a particularly slow queue. There are a number of people in front of you and the cashier is taking forever, you are late for lunch and very angry; not only that, a man in front of you is talking very loudly of the phone. Anyone is bound to get angry in such a scenario and this is the perfect time for this neat little trick.

So shift your concentration and look at something else - a plant in a corner, price tags of the products you have picked up, the print on the shirt the man in front of you is wearing, the color scheme of the walls, the television screen. Look and concentrate on these things as the queue moves along slowly, and don't let anything else bother you.

Trick #4: Pen down your Anger

This might not be possible in all the situations, but only when you are alone and no one is breathing down your neck. The moment you feel like you are getting angry, stop everything you are doing and grab something to write on - a pen and paper, or open a new document on your computer, or open a new note on your phone. Start writing!

It doesn't have to be a "Dear John" letter; what you need to do is to write whatever comes to your mind, something like:

"I can't take it anymore! If this person does not stop talking right now, I swear I am going to do something I am going to regret later. I may not even regret it later, that's how mad I am!"

Or, *"I wish I was anywhere but here! I wish I had never been born! Oh, how I wish I could do something drastic and not get the blame for it! I bet everyone around me will cheer if I can do half the things I am imagining! I wish... Oh, this is so frustrating!"*

Your entries don't have to make sense; neither do they have to be legible or accurate, because no one is reading them apart from you. The main point is for you to get the anger off your chest. So put all your rage into the paper, write whatever comes to your mind and never mind the content.

If you have been too bitter in your words, you can just

tear the paper or delete the document after you are done. You don't want anyone hearing what you wanted to say in anger, why would you want them to read about your thoughts?

Trick #5: Call a Loved One

If you don't want to write down your angst, you can just call up someone close to you and vent. Just pick up the phone and call someone you know will understand and be sympathetic, and not just point out your faults in the situation.

Be sure that you call the right person you can whine and throw a tantrum with, and not someone critical and unkind. Call someone with whom you can start the conversation with *"You can't believe the kind of day I have been having!"* and they'll know that you only want to talk. More importantly, the person you want to talk to needs to understand the main purpose you are calling - *that you want to get something off your chest, and not looking for advice or suggestions.*

You might just want to call a loved one for a chat, because listening to their voice makes you feel happier. Your partner, children or parents - just call them up and tell them that you love them, if you don't want to burden them with your problems.

It is always better to talk to a person who understands the problem or who has faced a similar situation, i.e. messaging a co-worker to complain about your boss, a married friend after a fight with your spouse, or to your sisters when you want to rant about your children. Talking to someone who understands will help you calm down better because, hey - there are other people with the same problem!

Remember one thing though: *you have to set a specific time limit for yourself for these sessions.* If you make a call for 5 minutes, stop your complaints immediately after the promised 5 minutes are up. Don't go on raving about the same problem for hours at an end even if you have all the time in the world. The moment your time is up, change the topic and talk about something else entirely.

Trick #6: Go to your "Happy" Place

Everyone should have a personal 'happy' place - an imaginary location and situation where they will be the happiest in their life. It could be on a relaxed vacation to the tropical islands, with plenty of sun and a drink in your hands, and nothing in the world to worry about; or, it could be in the largest library of the world, with millions of books to read at your leisure. Your 'happy' place is where you will be your most content, with nothing more that you need.

It's not mandatory that your happy place has to be somewhere you can only imagine and have never been. Rather, it could be the place you love the most in the world and often wish you could go back. Your parent's home, your grandparent's cabin you spent your summer vacations at, the city you went to on your honeymoon - the idyllic place where you were happy! It can also be your own home, surrounded by your partner and children, happy and carefree.

Next time you feel an angry outburst is about to surface, go down to your 'happy' place. It's not physically possible, but mentally you can travel thousands of miles in a second. You can visit your most favorite place in the world any time you want to, without the need for a visa, money or your luggage. Imagine what the sun felt like there, how hot or cold it was, how the Earth felt beneath your feet. Try to remember how you felt when you were actually there - the sights, the sounds and the smells.

Excuse yourself from where you are for a minute or two, and take a mini-vacation to your 'happy' place. There is a reason that place is named so; you will emerge happier and calmer. Any notion of an angry outburst would have long gone.

Trick #7: Get Yourself a New Affirmation

On the onset of an angry outburst? Choose a relevant affirmation and utter it again and again in your mind. Initially, you don't need to understand or realize the importance of what you are saying; you just need to say it - again and again, until you feel calmer.

You can choose one from these:

- *This TOO, shall pass.*

- *I am NOT going to give in.*

- *If I get angry, I LOSE.*

- Let it GO.

- I am BETTER than this anger inside me.

- I have the POWER.

- I WILL get over this.

- This is NOT who I am.

The next time you feel you are getting angry, choose the first affirmation that comes to your mind and start saying it again and again. You don't have to think too deeply about what you are saying, as long as your whole concentration is on these words. Try to emphasize on the words that are capitalized in the affirmations; this will help you feel more empowered even when you are feeling quite desolate.

You will slowly forget your anger as you keep muttering these words of wisdom. This is very much like a breathing exercise where, instead of breaths, you are using words to calm down. You will ultimately calm down, because words are powerful; and these are some very powerful affirmations that can help you feel energized and in control of yourself.

Trick #8: Make it Hilarious

There's an old trick that many speakers use before they go on a stage to speak in front of a crowd: *they imagine that the crowd is actually wearing nothing but their underwear.* The idea behind this is quite simple. We become very vulnerable when we stand in front of a large audience who is waiting for us to speak or perform. So, why not flip the situation and make the audience more vulnerable than we are? That is only possible by imagining them in their birthday suit - which is the most vulnerable a person can get!

This is actually a very controversial trick and many speakers find it crude and ineffective; not to mention, insulting to the audience. However, in some cases when you find yourself getting angry - this trick could actually work. You don't really have to imagine everyone in their underwear; you can borrow the concept and imagine other people in hilarious or embarrassing situations.

Boss shouting at you while everyone is staring? Quick - imagine your boss in a clown's outfit with a red rubber nose that s/he is honking with every other word. That's funny, right? Or imagine them in a pirate's costume with a parrot perched on one shoulder, and - what's this? The parrot seemed to have just pooped where it was standing. What a mess!

You get the general idea, right? Although, try and keep your fantasies to yourself. If you start smirking while your boss is giving you an earful, the consequences might not be too good. So imagine away anything you want to make of your boss, but keep your face straight and serious. You should look as if you are concentrating hard on the lecture being bestowed on you when in reality, you are trying out a rather hilarious trick to not get angry.

Trick #9: Stock up on your Favorite Snacks

What's your favorite snack? Something unhealthy and sinful, I'm sure. Whatever it is - a bar of Snickers or a cheese filled doughnut, keep one around you. This is your treat the next time you can successfully control your anger.

You see, this is an ingenious idea! The next time you start getting angry, you know you'll be getting a treat - your favorite snack. The anticipation of the snack alone will distract you as well as encourage you not to get angry. The moment you start getting angry, the thought of the upcoming snack will fill your mind, making it impossible for you to have an outburst.

Just like children get a treat when they behave, this is your treat for behaving the way you are supposed to. Think of it as a bribe or an encouragement not to get angry, or a reward - the result is the same every time. The trick is to stop your anger in its track, and the promise of your favorite snack is doing just that.

Trick #10: Take a Stroll

This is the best step there is to make sure that your anger doesn't get too much for you. On the onset of anger, excuse yourself from the situation and take a 5-minute walk. Now, this may not be possible if you are in the middle of a task or waiting in a queue, but very effective when you are in an argument. Especially when fighting with your partner, a good friend or a family member, taking a break for a few minutes and going for a walk can save you a lot of trouble later.

A walk will save you in more than one way: firstly, it will take you away from the situation. Usually, a fight ends in one or both parties accidentally saying something hurtful to each other in their anger, words that can never be taken back. Removing yourself from the situation takes away that chance of saying something wounding that you would have definitely regretted later.

Secondly, some timeout will help you cool off your anger. When you are too angry, your mind is extremely overworked. Anger doesn't give us the time to think about anything in a calm manner; it is an emotion that only reacts without any consideration. If we get even a few minutes to think when in the middle of an argument, we can realize how much we've said that we regret. If you don't get away from the scene when there's still time, you might not get the chance to save yourself from heartbreak later.

Thirdly, this 5-minute walk is also the perfect opportunity to think about how to recover from the damages you've caused from your brief anger outburst. Even if you have spent only a few minutes in an argument, there is bound to be some damage that your angry words or actions have caused. Thankfully you have left before you could have done more, but you would still need to apologize and make amends. These walks are the perfect opportunity to think about how to do so!

Walking away from anger is the perfect step you can take before your outbursts take a turn for the worst. Stopping anger in its tracks can be hard at first but with the right technique and enough will power, you will understand soon enough how to control your anger.

It's no use regretting and apologizing later, after you've had an outburst and hurt the people around you. What's indefinitely better is when you can recognize the onset of your anger and control yourself before it gets out of hand, saving yourself from disgrace and others from pain. These 10 tricks mentioned above in this chapter can help you in this matter - in stopping anger before this powerful and emotion harms your life to a great extent.

Dealing with Anger the Right Way

If you look again, the title of this book is not about hiding anger or suppressing it so that no one has any clue. This book, as the title suggests, is about managing anger - which is a much more healthy approach of dealing with anger.

It is not possible for a human being to never get angry in their life. The people who, according to others, never gets angry in their life may be considered a saint, but they also lead a troubled life. It's not that they don't get angry, but they suppress it within themselves, away from other people's eyes. This is certainly not healthy; these kind of people are bound to reach the limit of their tolerance one day and burst out - hurting themselves as well as their loved ones.

Similarly, the people who are always angry, or who gets angry at the slightest provocation, are also living a dangerous life. Through their frequent outbursts and furious attitude, they are harming themselves physically, mentally, emotionally as well as spiritually.

Smart are those people who know when to show their anger, how much to show, which medium to share their anger through and how not to hurt anyone else in the process. In other ways, they know the proper ways to channel their anger so that it transforms from a dangerous emotion to a powerful one.

Anger could be a destructive emotion, but it is sometimes a necessary one. This is not an emotion we should completely remove from our lives; neither should we suppress and hide anger. The best way to deal with anger is to channel it properly so that it becomes a productive and constructive force in our lives, and actually make our lives better. This is what this part of the book deals with - channeling your anger in a good way so that you neither have to feel ashamed by it or hide it from others.

Tip #1: Accept your Anger

Remember this tip: *you are allowed to get angry*. This tip is going to be an important one in your way to recovery. If you consider your frequent or excessive angry outburst a problem or an illness, it will be tough to help yourself. Rather, you need to accept your anger as a part of your behavior and personality, as a part of the person you are.

People all over the world are taught to control their anger from their childhood; this is a vice that needs to be hidden and never shown in public. Especially for women in many cultures, anger is considered to be a disgraceful emotion, not something to be exposed. These kind of advices throughout our life makes us view our anger as something negative and hateful, which becomes a problem because everyone eventually gets angry - some people more than others. Anger is as normal in a human being as any other emotion, but since we are always distrustful of it, our anger is exposed in two ways: *either we are fuming and violent, or we suppress it and show it passively.*

Neither one is the right path to take!

When our boss screams at us or someone deliberately cuts in front of us in a queue, we will get angry. The part where we 'get angry' is actually the normal side of our character and we need to accept that. Instead of thinking *"I shouldn't get angry!"* you need to accept what you are feeling

Yes, you are supposed to be angry because your boss is yelling at you in front of the whole office. You don't deserve to be treated like that because you are a good worker and a dedicated one. If your dedication goes unappreciated and results in an embarrassing situation like this, it is normal that you are angry!

The person who has cut in front of you should be the one feeling ashamed of their behavior, not you! The anger you would be feeling at that moment is completely normal. It's the careless behavior of the other person that is not right, and you should get angry about it. No need to check yourself; you are the one in the right here!

You need to allow yourself to feel your anger in such

situations, instead of automatically trying to suppress it. You need to accept the fact that anger is something that comes naturally to you; instead of fighting it, you need to acknowledge its presence. When you can calmly accept your anger, you won't have to suppress it, neither would you have to control it so that it doesn't take a hold over you.

So, the next time your boss is yelling at you when you know you don't deserve this kind of treatment, tell yourself *"Yes, I am angry because this is not the behavior I am entitled to. I am angry because this is embarrassing, and I don't have to take this anymore!"* Accept what you are feeling inside but don't suppress it; use that anger to take whatever step you need to. Explain yourself to your boss if you have to, or protest. Remove yourself from the scene if you don't want a confrontation then and there, or try the techniques described in the previous chapter to calm yourself down.

If someone has just stepped in front of you in a queue, by all means - do get angry! Don't try to hide your irritation, but don't just flare up as well. Accept the anger in you and protest, in a calm but resolute voice. Use your anger in this case; it won't work if you can't take advantage of your emotions the right way. Anger is a necessary and useful emotion at times; all it requires is for you to accept and recognize it in time, so that you can use it to improve your situation.

Tip #2: Let it Out

Okay, this technique will only help if you are home or in

a private place where other people won't be shocked with your behavior.

When you are extremely busy, trying to calm yourself won't work; it just won't, no matter how hard you try. In such situations, you need to let your anger out - but not on other people and expensive belongings! What you can do is scream - literally scream as loud as you can. Just go *"Aaaahh!"* or *"Why me?"* as loudly as possible and you can feel the tension leaving your body.

This is one of the most primal instincts of human being when angry, one that we always try to hide inside. Sooner or later, the instinct to scream and rant comes out in form of violence, self-harm and destruction. Isn't it better that we let it out the natural way if we have the opportunity? Try yelling when you are just too angry to calm yourself, but make sure that you are alone or in good company when you do.

Not a big fan of sound pollution? Try screaming into a pillow; this won't make much noise but still get the work done! Another technique for you to try is to punch a pillow - same relief, different approach. Just don't get so carried away that you end up with a room full of feathers and a ruined pillowcase.

Yes, you will certainly look like a spoiled child throwing a tantrum, but that's the beauty of it. Tantrums actually work. This is the reason that children can get extremely mad and then become fine in a few minutes - because they know the perfect outlet of anger. It's just us adults who take the unhealthy approach.

Tip #3: Get Down to Some Physical Action

This doesn't mean that you are allowed to punch someone or break something, but rather to choose an act that will engage you in some physical activities. A run or a hike sounds get - the perfect way to blow off some steam and to get fit at the same time! If you are a health conscious person, there's no better time to visit the gym than when you are angry.

Even a leisurely walk would do wonders, as described in the previous chapter. However, if you are really angry, on the verge of blowing up - something that requires strength is recommended. Try a physical activity that will require both your concentration and your strength, as well as passion.

Into sports? Great! This is the perfect time for some practice - when you are fuming mad and need something to fully grab your attention. I mean, when you are angry, why not use that emotion to get better at your sport of choice and get fit in the process?

Tip #4: Do Something Productive

Are you an imaginative person? Do you have a creative hobby that you enjoy? This is the perfect time to do something productive which you like.

The next time you are angry, try your hand at singing, dancing, writing or painting. These are productive outlets that will help you deal with anger better than screaming and punching into a pillow. Put all the emotion you are feeling into the task at hand and you will find yourself improving in your creativity.

Anger is a special emotion that has been the fuel behind a number of famous paintings and novels throughout history. Creative people are well-known for their passionate way of living life and anger is a trait that is common among many of them. Instead of letting this powerful emotion go to waste, they have channeled it to their creation and excelled. You can too!

Anger can be the push you need to put passion into your work; even if your creativity is just a hobby and not your profession, you can still excel in it if you choose to express yourself in a productive field.

Tip #5: Do What you Love

However useful anger is, it is also an emotion that makes you feel wretched - at least for the moment. Sometimes, it is hard to concentrate when you are feeling mad, and being creative is not an option for you. Apart from these activities, there must still be something that you love doing for yourself.

Take gardening, for instance. This is a great activity that requires attention to detail and time, and is the perfect way to keep you distracted. It can keep you fit too; being close to nature will definitely help you feel better in a refreshing way that is not possible indoors. If this is something you really enjoy, some personal time with your beloved plants and flowers can give you more happiness and release than any other activity.

Love cooking? Try something new - a recipe of a friend you've always loved and borrowed, or something downloaded from the Internet. Cooking is fun and is a consuming task; it is a great hobby, too and the end result would be delicious - or disastrous, depending on your skill level!

Baking sounds good too. If you have all the ready equipments at home, bake a cake!

Playing an instrument can be good way to deal with angry thoughts, especially something as forceful as drums or a guitar. Many talented musicians express their aggression through their music, and excel at it too. If you already play an instrument, you might be familiar with the feeling. If you don't play anything, this is the perfect excuse to choose an instrument and learn!

Reading and watching television are relatively tamer activities but you are most welcome to them if they work. Read your favorite book as a child, or watch a movie you've always loved; listen to some calming music - these are also great ways to calm yourself and make you see reason when you are angry.

Tip #6: Clean Your Home

This activity requires a special mention because it is one

of the best ways to deal with anger. When you have had a rough day at work and had been struck at traffic for a long time, coming home to a dirty and unkempt house could be the final strike of the match you needed for a full-blown angry outburst. Instead of slamming the door and leaving a room that is filling you with more anger than before, clean it.

Cleaning your home will help you in more than one way: *it will divert your focus from the reason you were angry in the first place.* While you are too busy to fold clothes, sweep and dust, you will gradually forget you were angry. Besides, this is an activity that requires you to get physical, making you sweat and move around a lot. It is my belief that cleaning is also very close to a form of exercise; it has all the same mechanisms working for it.

Finally, at the end of the day, you get the satisfaction of a clean house and a job well done. In a clean environment, it will be harder to get angry over small concerns. Rather, you will feel the need to congratulate yourself for finding a productive outlet for the rage you have felt on moments before.

Choose a chore that is physically demanding, like cleaning the toilet or vacuuming the whole house. If your home is already clean, don't let that stop you. Start your spring cleaning early and rearrange your whole wardrobe just for the sake of it. Sort out your DVD collection or books, and clean your kitchen cabinets.

On a final note, *doing your dishes may be the best household chore there is.* I'm not just making an assumption; there is a very valid scientific reason behind this. Doing your dishes involves running water, which creates negative ion in the air around you[13]. Despite the name, "Negative" Ions are actually molecules that help alleviate depression and stress. When you are in the proximity of running water, your mood can actually lift, i.e. when you are near a waterfall, the ocean or a river, or even in the shower. If you are feeling angry because you are in a bad mood or because you are feeling depressed, heading straight for the dirty dishes can be a great idea!

Tip #7: Take a Bath

A nice, relaxing bath doesn't only do wonders for your stress, but also your anger. Feeling irritated after a long day at work or after spending the whole day taking care of messy and disorderly children? A leisurely bath could do wonders for your mood.

If you are feeling mad with someone, or if an incident is bothering you - take a bath. Take an hour and soak yourself in a bath full of relaxing oils or salts, and watch as your anger melts away. Bring a good book with you if you want, or some good music; this could be also the perfect time for your one glass of drink at the end of the day.

I'm sure you've heard of the phrase *"Don't go to bed angry!"* With this tip, you won't have to. A bath before bedtime will help you forget all your day-long frustrations, anger and irritation. Similarly, taking a bath - or a long shower if a bath is not possible - can ensure a good start of the day.

Tip #8: Treat Yourself

It is important that you take care of yourself and treat yourself as often as possible, in whatever way you feel. Feeling unappreciated and unloved is a very big reason behind passive anger, especially in women. The best way to *not* feel like that is to pamper and love yourself, and to make yourself feel good.

The way you want to treat yourself is completely up to you; it can be a cup of coffee by yourself, a relaxing massage or a vacation. Browsing for books or watching a movie by yourself, or even planning to get away on a spa weekend - these are the things that will help you feel better.

Women in particular have trouble with their self-esteem; they spend all their time at work and in taking care of their children, with barely enough time left for themselves. This makes most women feel unappreciated, and often cranky, as they have no time to spend on themselves. Treating yourself often and in the way you like can help make you feel better and lighten any angry thoughts forming in your mind.

Treating yourself does not always involve spending money. You can find ways to feel pampered and rested by something simple that does not require money. How? Take a day off work and sleep the whole day away, especially after you've just completed a complicated and long project. Binge-watch your favorite TV series all day, with no one to distract you; meet your friends for a night-out and spend hours talking. Ask your partner to take care of your children while you curl up with a good book and a coffee, and not do anything all day. The main objective would be find some time for yourself to do something you like; spending money is just a way to do it.

Tip #9: Spend Time with a Loved One

No one can help you feel better than a loved one who understands. Due to the busy life we all lead, it is sometimes hard to spend some quality time with the people we love and cherish - our partners, parents, children, siblings and friends. These are actually the people who make us feel better about ourselves, not the smart phones we are always staring at or the virtual friends we feel more comfortable communicating with.

A feeling of isolation is common among the people who don't get to spend time with their loved ones. This is where we make a mistake, because these people are an extremely important part of our life. Not only spending time with them, but spending quality time, with our loved ones is crucial to our emotional health. This feeling of loneliness can lead to frustration and then to anger.

Spending quality time with a loved one does not mean going to the movies together, or going on a date night where everyone will be busy with their phones. Rather, this is what increases distance between two people - when they are together but not interested in communicating with each other. Quality time requires real conversations, where the phone is kept silent and there are no distractions around. You won't need to book an expensive vacation to feel close to a loved one; it is possible to communicate and have fun with each other in your own room.

This problem is more common in a relationship. Two people who are supposed to be the closest to each other slowly drift away, and the number of issues arise between them that are usually left unsaid. These unsaid issues later become the reason for angry outbursts, often leading to the end of the relationship. Couples need to be comfortable enough with each other to be able to share everything, so that there is no chance of misunderstanding and anger.

Not only in a romantic relationship but in all types, it is important to keep the road to communication open. When two people can really talk to each other - about their hopes and inspirations, their failures and fears, their plans for the future, there will never be any issues for anger between them.

So the moment that you start feeling angry with a loved one, talk to them. Tell them what's bothering you and what you want to change, directly; there's nothing better than direct communication to help lessen frustration and anger in a person.

Tip #10: Spend Some Relaxed Time Every Day

Certain relaxation techniques are great for calming down when you feel like you are getting angry suddenly. However, that's not all that relaxation methods are good for;

rather, meditation, reflection, prayer and other relaxation techniques should be made a regular part of our lives.

This is especially important for the people who are always angry, always cranky. They are the ones who need to dedicate at least half an hour of their day, every day, to a relaxation techniques to feel better.

What can relaxation techniques achieve? Well, for starters, will calm your restless mind. In some passive form of anger, the mind becomes fidgety; whatever we try to concentrate on, our thoughts go back to what is bothering us.

Suppose for any reason, you have been late to work for three days in a row, which is rare for you because you are always at time. However if you hear someone comment on how you are *always* late to work, this is definitely going to get you mad. You can't really protest at that particular moment because you have actually been late recently, and neither can you silently accept the comment made on you. These are the situations where your mind will become restless and angry because you can't immediately control or better the situation; at least, not until you've regained your former reputation as someone who is never late.

This kind of anger will remain inside you - not in a dangerous amount, but like a small flame burning constantly. You will eat, sleep and wake up with this anger inside you, nipping at you every now and then. If you don't calm yourself, this small but passionate anger will one day grow up to be a big one, and you will start hating the person who made that comment, or the workplace that didn't appreciate you!

Relaxation techniques are crucial when you want to calm yourself from the inside and not show any anger. Not just a few minutes of it when you are feeling angry, but every day when you wake up in the morning. This should be a part of your daily morning ritual, 10 minutes spent apart where you prepare for the day ahead. If you have woken up fidgety and angry about what happened a week ago, relaxing for only a few minutes will help you calm yourself.

Relaxation techniques don't have to be limited to the beginning of the day only. Rather, these techniques are short and easy and can be tried anywhere and anytime - while you are commuting (but not when you are driving), at lunch break, while watching television, in the middle of work, etc. All you need is some time to yourself and no distractions, and you can come out of a mini relaxation procedure feeling refreshed and good as new. None of these techniques require more than 5 minutes or any equipment.

There are a number of easy but effective meditation and relaxing techniques that even beginners can master very quickly. A few of them are described in detail at the end of this book.

If you have had anger issues for what feels like forever, it is going to take a little time to bring your emotions under control. You can't just wake up one day and decide not to get angry anymore; that's not how anger management works. Rather, you have to take it slow, practice every step of the way so that things and incidents that used to aggravate you before loses their power. This may be a slow process, but it is an effective one.

What Not to Do When Angry

There may be a hundred tips on what to do when angry in this book, but you also need to keep in mind the things you are not allowed to do. It is indeed difficult to keep these points in mind when you are fuming mad, but they will save you a lot of heartaches later.

When we are angry, all the thoughts that come to our minds are of violence and hatred. What we say hurts others and what we do harms the people we love. If we are just a little bit careful in our anger, we can refrain from doing some permanent damage to our lives. It's the words we utter and our accidental actions that takes our rage to a level we never intended to reach in our anger.

So try to keep these few words of advice in mind the next time you are angry, and you won't have to regret your bouts of anger too much.

Rule #1: Don't Go to Bed Angry

This is an age-old rule that is still true today: *going to bed angry will only make matters worse.* This is not just an advice to a married couple but for everyone else who is angry – with themselves, with their family members, with their careers and friends, and with their life.

So what happens when you go to bed still feeling angry? First of all, you won't get enough sleep. Sleep doesn't come easy to a restless and agitated mind; chances are, you will end up tossing and turning all night long. When it's finally time to get up in the morning, your brain will be fuzzy and your thoughts will still be disturbed. You will spend the whole day feeling worse than you had when you were actually angry. This will add to your existing anger and make you crankier, and you will go home feeling angrier than before. The fight that will follow will most probably be bigger with worse consequences.

Besides, it is always better to finish up an argument before retiring for the night. Otherwise, there will be a thousand things unsaid which will cluster your mind throughout the night, making you make the situation worsen manifold in your thoughts. You won't be able to say the things you are thinking and that makes matters more serious. When you go to bed without resolving the matter, your ego wins the round against your love for the other person.

Finally, there's actual scientific proof that going to bed angry and with an agitated mind actually harms your mental health. According to a study[14] conducted by the University of Massachusetts, the emotions felt immediately before sleep is actually enhanced while a person is sleeping. This is a step taken by the brain in order to preserve the memories and the feelings experienced throughout the day as we retire for the night. If we go to bed with negative emotions – in this case, anger and resentment – you will wake up the next day feeling even angrier.

Rule #2: Don't Deny Your Anger

When you are fuming mad, don't keep denying it. This is something almost every other person does; they deny their anger and name it something else.

I'm not angry; I am just surprised that you don't understand me.

Of course I am not angry at you; I am just disappointed in you!

It's not anger I am feeling, just shock at your behavior.

No, I am not angry; humiliated and embarrassed maybe.

This is a strategy we all adopt sometimes – hiding our anger behind some other emotions. However, by denying our anger and repressing it behind shock, misunderstanding and pain, we are actually delaying our reaction to it. We are telling ourselves we are not angry, rather than to the other person; this little game of 'hide and seek' is being played with our own feelings more than with someone else.

Don't deny your emotions when you are obviously angry. When you do that, you are only lying to yourself; you are actually avoiding confrontation with your real emotions because you are afraid of the consequences. This is not the right path to take if you are looking forward to controlling your anger. Accepting your anger is the first step to recovery, and something you need to be completely honest about if you want to succeed in this journey.

Rule #3: Don't Drive

This is probably the worst thing you can do when angry: *take your car out for a drive*. Drivers who are angry are prone to take more risks on the road; they are more aggressive and cause more accidents wherever they are. When angry, you are - by nature - in the mood for violence and in absence of control, you are likely to cause an accident. So if you are feeling angry, stay away from driving. Ask someone else to give you a lift, or opt for public transport for the days you are in a bad mood.

According to a number of studies on the subject, it has been deduced that extreme anger gives a person 'tunnel vision'. They see only what is directly in front of them, as if driving through a tunnel. In their anger, they are blind from everything that is happening around them, outside their field of vision. This is one of the main reasons they tend to hit other cars beside them, cars coming from the other side, or trees by the road.

A counseling psychologist from Colorado State University, Jerry Deffenbecher, conducted a research[15] based on more than 10,037 police reports to arrive at his conclusions. According to him, the majority of angry drivers have some special characteristics present in their behavior:

> *They will be judgmental of the other drivers on the road and use offensive language and gesture towards them, even when there are children in those vehicles;*

They will think of physically harming the other drivers on the road and damaging their vehicles;

They will show the tendency to take risks on the road, i.e. switch lanes recklessly, speed and disregard a red signal.

They will honk more often and more forcefully, yell at the other drivers on the road and get angry within a second without any serious reason.

They will appear to be more anxious and impulsive on the road;

They will be more prone to accidents and mishaps.

There's a special word for the particular kind of anger seen among drivers: *road rage!* According to a survey by AAA[16] on July 2016, more than eight million people in the USA have shown examples of road rage at least once over a period of 12 months. More than 104 million drivers have purposefully tailgated another driver and about 5.7 million drivers have deliberately bumped their car into someone else. *[Source: newsroom.aaa.com]*

So that settles it – *don't drive when you are mad!*

Rule #4: Don't Make Drastic Declarations

Drastic declarations are accidental when angry, but they have the power to seriously hurt someone close to you. A fight with your partner or spouse can lead to someone yelling *"I want a divorce!"* or *"I want to break up with you!"* Although these declarations are almost never serious, they can hurt a relationship and create barrier between two people.

Similarly, there are some other phrases that we use carelessly but which can really hurt someone on the receiving end of it.

"I wish I've never met you!"

"Why don't you go away and die already?"

"I regret the day I fell in love with you."

"I knew I was making a mistake in marrying you."

"How I wish you have never been born."

"You've ruined my whole life just by being in it."

These are the kind of announcements that we blurt out in anger and almost never mean it. Nevertheless, they can severely hurt the people who listen to these comments because we are not careful with our words.

Even if some rude comments like these come to your mind in extreme anger, you need to curb your tongue and control them. Tell yourself to keep these declarations for later when you are capable of logical thoughts instead of when you are fuming, because the words spoken in anger are never what your heart wants to say.

Rule #5: Don't Answer Emails or Texts

Sometimes emails from a colleague or a boss – making accusations or blaming you – make you mad, and you feel like replying with an equally rude email to the person. This is where things can get really complicated at work if you reply to official emails while angry. Of course your tone will be rude, your words chosen with care to hurt the person you are angry with. What happens if the person you are writing to is your boss or someone very important to your organization? Your job might be at risk.

A lot of negative emotions is always present in a workplace; there are people from all walks of life who work together to build up a successful workforce. If your colleagues are not all your friends, they deserve respect and understanding from you. Replying to an accusatory email with an even ruder one disturbs the balance of the workplace and puts your own career in jeopardy. Don't let your first reaction to such an email be sending a rude response in reply, especially if you don't want to put your job at risk.

So what should you do? After the initial reaction, wait before you start replying. Read the email again; there could be a number of issues you are missing:

If the mail goes straight to a point without a "Hello" or "Hi", it might be an email sent in a hurry and the person has no idea he is being rude;

If too many capital letters has been used, which actually means the person is yelling the words, it might be that the person has no idea what capital letters signify in an email;

Maybe this person has trouble communicating through words when they are extremely polite and friendly in person;

It a certain word of phrase is making you angry, it might be that the person who has sent you the mail doesn't know the meaning of that word or how it affects you;

Perhaps the excessive use of "????" and "!!!!" wasn't meant to be rude or condescending, but used to emphasize a point.

Even after everything, if the mail is still rude, it doesn't mean you should send back an equally rude answer. Take your time to compose a reply if that helps, and then save it as a draft until you are able to think with a clear mind. If the email needs immediate reply, send an acknowledgement email rather than a reply and delay the matter a few minutes. At the end of the day, you are going to be thankful you hadn't sent an angry reply because you were tempted to. Just delaying the moment will give you the time to think more calmly and send a more rational reply.

The same goes for informal texts between friends. If someone's text makes you mad, don't reply in an aggressive and rude manner; it may ruin the relationship between you. Take your time or excuse yourself for the moment if you value your bond with the other person you are texting. Angry texts are just as bad as rude emails, and they have the power to forever destroy your friendships.

Rule #6: Don't Go Public on Social Media

This is a rather annoying habit that some people have; they go and rant about their personal conflicts on Social Media sites. Every day Facebook, Twitter and Instagram is flooded with stories of people breaking up, fighting with parents and partners and drifting apart from their friends. In their anger, too, people share rude comments about people they are mad about, or indirect comments on how they are feeling.

This is not a good practice – to share intimate and personal details with the public. Chances are, your conflict will end and you will stop being angry with the person, but by then, the whole world would know what's happening in your life. Besides, you are invading someone else's personal life when you are sharing your anger with the public – something the other person might not like.

Any kind of conflict between two people needs to be solved in person, face-to-face and direct. Sharing your anger in a rude status will only invite unwanted inquisitors into your personal life, and make you a laughing stock. So refrain from this habit, because it is not a good way to solve the problem. Sharing on social media sites does not help you in any way; only direct communication can solve the problem.

Rule #7: Don't Eat when Angry

People who eat when angry are people who overeat. For many people, eating does not only mean satisfying hunger, but to mask some other feelings deep down inside. This could be profound sadness someone is hiding, or pain and anger. There are many people around the world who use food as a comfort when they are trying to deal with some powerful emotion, anger being one of them.

There is a special term for the condition where people seek refuge in food: *binge eating*. Binge eating is an almost uncontrollable period of eating triggered by a powerful emotion – anger, depression or anxiety. The person who has the tendency to binge eat, at times, shows unnatural hunger for unhealthy food that only passes when the emotion itself is gone. A person who has always been health-conscious can lapse in judgment and eat the food they would never do in a normal situation. Binge eating is an almost uncontrollable urge, and in a very little time, a person can make more unhealthy choices than they have made an entire year.

A number of situations can trigger this uncontrollable need to eat.

You've just had a fight with your spouse, and the only thing that is going to comfort you is ice cream, a whole tub full of it, followed by two more!

After a heated exchange of accusatory emails with a colleague, you feel absolutely exhausted and automatically reach for a large bar of chocolate; when it's finished, you go down to the newspaper stand and get 10 more!

The traffic from work was exhausting; you had to suppress your desire to scream at a lot of other drivers and when you are almost home, you stop at the deli and pick up a large piece of chocolate cake, and then an assortment of cupcakes – a whole box of them for yourself.

After a heated breakup, you pick up the phone to call your best friend to vent with a twelve-pack box of doughnuts, which you finish by yourself.

People have the tendency to make unhealthy choices in

food when angry. No one really reaches for an apple or a salad when they are fuming mad, but something fried, fattening and filled with sugar. It is the unhealthy and delicious foods that call to us when we are angry, and we end up consuming a lot more than we are used to. The person who would always refuse sugar in their coffee would finish up a whole slice of chocolate cake without even realizing the damage they are causing to their body. Even if they do realize, they can't stop themselves!

Don't reach for food when you are angry; don't even stay in the vicinity if you can. Control and engage yourself with someone more physical that will drain you but not damage your health. Take a walk, away from all the tempting food. Remove yourself from your favorite deli where you know you might be tempted; leave the kitchen and not look back. When angry, there's no room for *"Just a small piece"* or *"only a bite"*. If you start on a tub or ice cream, you won't be able to stop until you have finished every drop of it.

Besides, the food won't make you feel better, even if it feels that way for the moment. Rather, when you are finally done eating, you will feel even angrier with yourself for giving into your urges. Hunger doesn't play an important role in binge eating; it's all in your mind.

Even if you are actually hungry, wait until you have your anger in control to eat. It is almost impossible that you will be able to make healthy food choices in your anger, so don't give yourself the chance.

Rule #8: Don't Drink Too Much, Either

This is another bad choice that people make sometimes: reach for a drink after an angry outburst or a heated argument in order to calm down. Some people drown their sorrow in drinks; others drink to hide their anger. In both cases, alcohol worsens the situation rather than improving our moods.

The theory of binge eating also applies when it comes to alcohol. You won't be able to stop yourself after the first drink, but reach for more until you have consumed more alcohol under an hour than you do in a year. Before you know it, you'll find yourself getting drunker and drunker, still unable to stop.

Besides, alcohol is well-known for lowering inhibitions in a person; it doesn't only mean that you become braver, but that you also become more aggressive and more confident. You will start to argue more even when you are in the wrong, often becoming abusive and violent in the process. This is definitely not the best time to communicate with anyone, least of all the person you are angry with.

Too much anger can also lead to violent behavior, leading you to do something extreme you are going to regret later. It is the combination of alcohol and extreme anger that makes a raging person dangerous – lure them into harming others and destroying possessions, and saying things they would have never uttered if sane. When drunk, no one has the capability to think about the consequences of their actions and words. They can damage property and lives without a single thought, and this is what makes drinking while angry a deadly combination.

Rule #9: Don't be Around Expensive and Breakable Objects

Anger and breaking things always go hand in hand, whether it is something expensive lying around, your phone or your glasses. Angry people seem to find a vicious kind of joy in damaging possessions that they have always loved. This trait is more prominent in men than in woman, mainly because men by nature have more aggressive manners than their female counterparts.

When we are angry, we start thinking with our primitive instincts, not by the rules forced on us by society. People go back to their fundamental need of destroying something to feel in control when angry. The sound of breaking and crashing helps too; hence the repeated occurrence of slamming doors and throwing away plates when a person is angry.

Breaking something, especially something that is going to shatter into pieces and make a lot of noises – mirrors and satisfies the anger inside us. It is almost impossible to stop us from destroying valuable possessions when we are viciously angry. The next best thing would be to remove ourselves from the location where possessions are at a risk. If you are at work and anger sets in, remove yourself from your computer – and any other electronic gadgets – before you harm them. If you are at home and need to show your anger, punch a pillow!

Rule #10: Don't Make Important Decisions

Extreme and uncontrollable anger is not the time to make life-changing decisions; when you are angry, you are not thinking straight and hence, not in the right state of mind to decide anything. If you end up quitting your job because of a heated argument with a colleague or breaking up with someone after a fight – you might end up regretting it. Even if those are the right decisions to make, you need to make them on a sound and calm mind, not when you are furious.

Decision made in haste and in anger are never good ones; most of the time, you will end up regretting and trying to reverse what you have done. So yes, compose a letter of resignation if that makes you feel better, but don't email it if you are not 100% sure of your decision; write someone a hateful letter to vent your anger but destroy it immediately. Whatever you do, don't make a hasty decision that you won't be able to reverse later, like leaving a hateful voice mail for someone you had a fight with or destroying your partner's possessions after a breakup. You're going to have a hard time amending the situation if you do!

Rule #11: Don't Try to Socialize

When you are feeling angry, it is definitely not the time to attend a party and socialize. To communicate with people, especially remote acquaintances and strangers – need a lot of concentration and patience, virtues which are absent in an angry person.

In anger, the best company to have is that of good friends or family members who can help you cope with your emotions. People around you should be ones who won't judge you based on your words and behavior, but try to help you. When you are furious and in a social gathering, your comments would come out as sarcastic and rude, creating misunderstanding.

If you need to talk to someone, talk to someone you can trust – a friend, your partner, a sibling. You shouldn't share your feelings and opinions with everyone you know; chances are, you will face ridicule, pessimism and blank stares from other people who are not close to you. Keep your thoughts for people who care about you, because they are the ones who can actually help.

Rule #12: Don't Return to Discarded Bad Habits

It takes a lot of willpower to let go of a bad habit – smoking, swearing, excessive drinking, binge eating or doing drugs; anger is the perfect time to lose control and revert to these bad habits. Someone who has given up smoking will always look for cigarettes when angry; an alcoholic on the mend will crave a drink. This is the most vulnerable time in a person's life when they are at the risk of falling back on an old habit they have worked hard to fight. Once you give into the temptation, it will be harder for you to let go.

It will take all your self-control to not look for a smoke

or a drink when you are hungry, if those are the bad habits you have conquered. It will not be easy task, but if you truly want to control your anger, you have to refuse yourself every single time.

Anger is one of the most powerful emotions known to man, one that can completely change us in a moment. It is in our anger that we can do the most harm – to ourselves and to the people we love. Besides controlling anger, it is important that we also know of the activities we should avoid at all costs when angry; otherwise, we might end up losing the people who really matter and opportunities that might never come back.

Where to Channel your Anger

Harmful as anger is, it can actually be a pretty usual emotion when needed. It can be the motivation you were looking for, the push you needed to finally stand up and fight. Anger can be repressed, shown or vented, but anger can also be channeled into another aspect of your life where it is needed more.

So, where can you channel your anger where it can be more useful?

Into Your Work

Fed up with watching your colleagues get promoted and bonuses, it is normal that you will feel angry and unappreciated. No matter how hard you work, you seem to lack the proactive attitude that your colleagues have, and you are left behind while they succeed. You can behave in one of two ways if this happens: *you can sit back and watch the same thing happen to you year after year, or you can get your anger to motivate you.*

Use the anger you feel to motivate you; the new you will not lose a single opportunity to shine at your workplace. Instead of wallowing in your anger and jealousy, put all your focus into finding out what your organization needs. Think and come up with new ideas to pitch, and be proactive in your role at work. Even when you are not absolutely sure, share your ideas with your boss; you never know when one of them might be a hit!

You have to make your colleagues notice and respect you. If you are stuck at a job where you are neither appreciated nor happy, life will become very dull for you. You will spend all day frustrated and go home angry, and all your negative emotions will fall on your family members. Instead of spending your years like this, use the anger inside you to make a change at your workplace.

Into Your Business

How many times has this happened? Frustrated in a dead-end job with no future, someone quits to open their own business and BOOM! After a few years of dedication and hard work, they have a successful business on their hands.

If this has happened to someone else, it can happen to you too. If you find yourself frustrated at your job, angry at your life and distrustful of the future, maybe it is time to plan something else. We all deserve to do something we love and perhaps your anger is telling you to quit your job and try something else.

Success is the best revenge you can take on someone. If there's someone you want to prove yourself to, there's nothing better than to build a successful business of your own. If this is what you want in life, get down to it. Use the pent up anger inside you to work hard and succeed – that'll be the best revenge you can take on people who have always unappreciated and troubled you before!

Into Your Education

In almost every high school movie ever made, there are two types of students – *the jocks and the nerds.* The nerds are usually bullied, teased and laughed at because they are different from others. However, it is the nerds who are typically the studious ones who go on to win scholarships and get accepted into good colleges. I believe it is the anger in them, the frustration built up from being mocked and bullied, that pushes them to put their heart and soul into their education. This is their revenge on the people who have bothered them throughout the years, made their life miserable.

Didn't get accepted into the college of your dreams? Don't just be sad; use the anger inside you to get into better colleges the next semester by studying more and trying harder. Put your frustration and rage to better use instead of breaking your possessions and being rude to people. Exposing your anger may make you feel better for the moment, but using it correctly will change your life forever.

Into Your Health

Physical exercise is the perfect way to deal with anger – sudden or chronic. So if you find yourself getting angry every now and then, use it to become fit. Do something physically draining whenever you are angry – walking, jogging, running or beginner's exercise and you will become fitter day by day.

Make your local gym your regular place to deal with your anger issues. Instead of ranting and screaming, exercise until you drain your emotions. Convert your anger into adrenaline to exercise better and to get something positive in your life.

There are a lot of aspects of your life where you can use your pent-up anger to bring positive changes into your life. So find out the part of your life that is missing something and change it for the better. You have all this energy built up inside you; use it well!

Living With an Angry Person

It is never easy to live with someone who is always angry, who can flare up any time at the slightest provocation, and who can become violent and aggressive any moment. It is mostly a partner or a spouse who has to deal with this problem more than anyone else; in some cases, children. The partners and the children are the people who have to live with an angry person every day and deal with their anger issues.

Many people who have grown up in an angry household – where both or one parent was constantly angry, abusive and violent - will show signs of anger themselves at some point of their life. The people who live with them, i.e. their partners and spouses, as well as children, will also eventually start showing the same symptoms, indicating another angry generation. This is indeed a vicious cycle that needs to be solved at the root.

Before that, it is important to know how to live with a person who has anger issues.

Advice #1: Don't Take their Words Personally

An angry person is going to say a lot of things, some of them really insulting and hurtful. However, if this is a regular habit of this person, don't take the words personally. 95% of what they say when angry is just the anger talking. Although it doesn't justify their behavior, you need to understand that the words used in anger aren't something the person would have said when sane.

Don't ignore their rant when they are talking, but don't take the words to your heart. Go through the scene as if you are watching a movie, a silent spectator who is not involved. Unless the person is being extremely abuse, stay close; observe but don't participate. If the situation worsens to where you can no longer just sit back and listen, leave.

Before reaching that point, disengage yourself from whatever they are saying and let the words simply wash over you.

Remember: *it's their vulnerability talking, not them.* The person who is screaming and insulting you is actually the one who is scared. They are hiding their vulnerability behind their anger and trying to hurt you so that you can't hurt them. As long as you manage to ignore their words, they won't have any power over you. You are just a medium for them to express their anger, just because they are angry; it doesn't necessarily mean they are angry at you. They could be reacting to a completely different stimuli but directing their anger at you.

Advice #2: Don't Feel the Need to Reply Every Time

Even if you are at the receiving end of rude comments and insults, you don't need to response to each and every one of them. What you need to do is to be around them, listen to them and silently support them the best you can.

If you try to answer all their queries or counter-attack their insults, it will take the angry person longer to cool down. Instead of automatically cooling down in a few minutes, it will turn into a full-fledged argument that can go on for hours. Try and limit yourself to single-syllable answers if you want the outburst to be over quickly; if you end up getting angry and join in the explosion, matters will worsen.

Advice #3: Understand their Reason

Try to see past the anger into the reason; find out the reason behind the anger and you will understand it. They may be angry over a missed deadline, trouble at work, the illness of a loved one, financial trouble, or something reasonable. Their method of expressing may not be correct but their anger can have valid reasons behind it, which you need to identify and understand.

Understanding the reason behind someone's anger is very important in order to help them. Once you do that, you can be calm enough to try and find a solution. Otherwise, it's not easy being on the receiving point of anger if you take the words personally and get angry yourself. When you realize the person in front of you is angry about a completely different matter and only taking it out on you, you can be unbiased enough to help.

Advice #4: Don't Drag the Past into It

Even if you do get involved into the argument, be careful not to drag past incidents into it. This is a trait found more in women than in some men – they bring up topics that were all solved in the past, which ultimately lengthens the argument and makes it more serious.

In order to defeat the other person, don't bring up examples of past failures and disappointments. This might aggravate them more and worsen the outburst, as the person was already furious to begin with. The best strategy to deal with an angry person would be to remain silently (almost) supportive and caring; if you do get involved in the argument, keep your comments related to the-then current disagreement, not something from the past that is a sore point.

Advice #5: Show That you Understand

When the other person is ranting and fuming, you have to pay attention and listen to what they are saying, as well as what they are not saying. They may seem furious about the traffic on the way home, but actually worried about meeting a deadline that needs to be submitted the next day. Listening will give you a clear idea about what is really bothering the person in front of you.

It's great that you understand the problem, but you have to show them that you understand and that you are sympathetic. Not just random mumblings of *"I know"* or *"I would be too"* which could mean anything. You need to be clear and specific, so that they know they have a friend around to rely on.

I can understand how frustrating it must have been, stuck in traffic for so long when you have work pending. Frankly, I would have been angrier if I were you!

Doesn't this sound much better than:

So you were stuck in traffic. What's new about that? I get that too, you know, and I don't lose my mind!

Even if you think the person is overreacting, try and be sympathetic. The right words of support will help them feel understood and supported, and they will eventually calm down. It is no wonder the Bible says: "A gentle answer turns away wrath, but a harsh word stirs up anger." (Prov.15:1)

Advice #6: Don't Make it About Yourself

When you are dealing with an angry person, it is all about them. Even when you are at the receiving end and hearing insulting comments, don't make it about you. If this is someone who loves you but is extremely angry at the moment, they will regret their actions later.

Not even in your mind, should you make everything about yourself. If the other person is rambling on and on about a colleague, who is making their life miserable, accept that it is the actual reason behind their anger. Don't jump to conclusions where you are the main culprit and the reason behind their anger.

"It must be me. I have never seen him/her so angry before! I must be making his/her life a misery!"

"I know s/he isn't saying it, but I am the one responsible for the unhappiness in him/her."

This is something many of us do and it can make the matter at hand worse in two ways. First of all, you are unnecessarily blaming yourself when it's not your fault at all; you might start imagining reasons behind the anger that do not exist. While the other person may actually be angry about someone cutting in front of them in a queue, you are worried about the state of your relationship/marriage which you are sure is making them unhappy.

Secondly, voicing such concerns will make the other person feel misunderstood and misheard. Here they are, frustrated about some form of injustice they have just experienced and you have managed to make it all about you. This is actually one of the biggest problems that couples face in their life together: *instead of seeing each other as individuals, they make it all about themselves as a duo.*

Don't do that; try to look at the situation as it is. If the person who is angry says they are frustrated about a deadline, don't make it about your relationships.

This is actually also common among parents, as well. If their children seem angry more often, they jump to the conclusion that they have failed as parents, instead of looking for the real reasons. They blame themselves for not spending enough time together, of working late or hiring help to take care of children – anything but the real reason. As a result, the children feel isolated and misunderstood, with no one around to solve their real reasons.

Advice #7: Keep Yourself Safe

Above everything else, keep yourself safe. If the person who is angry suddenly seems violent, leave the scene without a second thought. In extreme anger, people can resort to anything, and you need to leave if the situation indicates something like this. Don't try to stop them, especially if this is someone bigger than you in size; just leave and wait, or get help somewhere else.

Even if their insults are getting too much for you, leave the scene. Cut yourself some slack if you can't handle the situation; tell yourself you've tried your best and failed. If this is a grown-up you are dealing with, they are not your responsibility. The important thing is that you have tried your best, and that's what matters.

If this is a regular occurrence in your life – the person getting angry often and regularly – the best step would be to seek professional help. No matter how much you try, or how hard the person in question tries – some situations require help from people who understand the problem and know how to deal with them.

Part 3: Seeking Professional Help

After you have tried your best, it is time for the professionals to help you and your family.

Anger is a very complex emotion; often, it is difficult to understand even when everything is happening to you. It is hard to draw the line between normal anger – which is actually a healthy approach of dealing with stress and frustration, and out-of-control anger.

Most of the time, we don't realize when we have anger issues. Anger becomes a trait in us, and people around us, people who love and care about us - parents, siblings, friends and spouses - become accustomed to our angry outbursts. Just like any other personality trait, anger becomes a part of us, even uncontrollable anger.

It's not until something drastic has happened that we finally realize something is wrong and that we need all the help we can get. So when should we seek professional help to control our anger, and what can we expect from counselors and therapists who are going to help us?

That's what we are going to discuss in this part of the book.

Before Asking for Help

Before we head off towards a professional's office, we need to get our homework done. Yes, you heard it right! You need something concrete to discuss with your counselor other than declaring *"I get angry a lot!"*

This includes you knowing exactly how your anger works – what makes you angry, how often do you get mad, and what do you do when mad. You can save a lot of time – both yours and your therapists – if you have the answers ready.

So before you seek professional help, you need to prepare two things: *an anger diary and an anger questionnaire.*

An Anger Diary

Yes, this is a diary – a virtual one or a physical one – that you need to carry around with you and write on every time you get angry or have an outburst. This could be the diary you write about your feelings every time you experience anger, or just a place you document the times you have an outburst. Following this for about a two to four weeks can be enough, especially if you have a tendency to get mad ever other day.

A good anger diary, written in any style, should at least have these features:

Date and time where you experienced anger

Location

The main incident, i.e. what happened to make you angry

Your initial reaction

Your feeling at that moment

Your rating for that anger/outburst (on scale of 1 to 10)

How long your outburst lasted

How you managed to cool down

Maintaining a diary with this information can help your therapist understand your anger, your triggers, as well as the approach to take to assist you. When you actually talk to a professional, you won't have to think about examples; your complete anger history for a month will be ready with you to discuss.

An Anger Questionnaire

This is similar to an anger diary which will also be helpful to a therapist. Unlike an anger diary where you are documenting your anger history, a questionnaire is basically an assessment of your feelings and reactions.

Like in any other questionnaire, you will need to answer a few questions, such as these below. This is a simple one; your therapist may give you another questionnaire to answer during therapy:

ANGER QUESTIONNAIRE:

(Answer yes or no to each question.)

_____ Do you show anger for everything that makes you mad?

_____ Do other people mostly annoy you?

_____ Do you get angry about things that have happened to you in the past?

_____ Do you often have trouble falling asleep thinking about everything that has made you angry all day?

_____ Do you have trouble forgiving people?

_____ Do you have trouble letting go of an issue?

_____ Do you stay awake at night thinking of replies you could have given but didn't when you were angry with someone?

_____ Do you often find yourself angry with your family members and close friends?

_____ Do you get angry when things don't go the way you want them to?

_____ Do you have trouble recalling things you said or did when you were angry?

_____ Do you regret your words or action later when you are not angry?

_____ Do you turn to unhealthy food, alcohol or cigarettes when you are angry?

_____ Do you usually feel alone and isolated?

_____ Do you feel disgusted with yourself after you have an angry outburst?

_____ Do you always want to physically hit the people you are angry with?

_____ Do you find yourself plotting revenge on other people who have hurt you?

_____ Do you feel violent enough to actually kill someone when angry?

_____ Do you have suicidal tendencies after an outburst?

If you have answered affirmative to most of these questions, it is definitely time to see a professional. Especially if you have said "yes" to the last four questions, there's no time to lose. You need professional help as soon as possible before you do something drastic that can ruin your life forever.

Anger Management Therapy

Realizing you have anger issues and need help is the first step to recovery. Reading this book, coming this far and thinking about getting professional help – they all mean that you have already started your journey towards improvement.

The first steps of controlling anger depend on you and you alone. You have to start trying to manage your anger, by all the techniques, tips and advices described in the second part of the book – Managing your Anger. If you are an angry person with normal outbursts, you can manage to control yourself. Especially with adequate physical exercises, creative activities and the support of your loved ones, you can learn to be in command of your anger when the time arises.

If you have a violent streak in you or if you physically want to harm someone in your bouts of outbursts, you need the help of a professional counselor to control yourself. A therapist can help you in two ways: *by helping you identify the reason behind your anger, and by teaching you a number of techniques to control your anger.*

This can happen either in a group or in a one-on-one session, depending on the severity of your condition and your requirements.

Anger Management: Group Therapy

In most of the cases, people who go to therapists for help

are dubious of group sessions, mainly because they aren't comfortable talking about what they consider to be a personal problem. However, group sessions are surprisingly effective and the whole experience turns out to be a rewarding one for most of the people who attend them.

Group therapy[17] is especially beneficiary for people who are in denial of their problem. These are the cases where the family and friends of an angry person seek help from a professional because the person in question doesn't admit to having a problem with anger. In a group session where other people share their experiences with the same problem, the person in question – who thinks their issues with anger is a normal one – can be surprised by the revelations.

Anger Management group sessions are exactly like they are portrayed in movies and television; they are available everywhere and just a phone call away for your convenience. Each group has one therapist and around 8-15 members. Each group meets once or twice a week, usually for about an hour or more; these sessions continue for 2-3 months for a total of 12 to 15 meetings.

The role of a therapist is almost limited in these sessions; it is mainly the patients themselves who talk and offer suggestions. The therapist only asks a few thoughtful questions to get the members talking and encourages them to express their feelings. It is the members who become each other's friends and confidants, and helps them throughout the sessions.

While some people are uncomfortable in the beginning to share their personal disaster stories, it gets easier over time with the support and encouragement from other members of the group who have gone through similar situations in life. The stories and experiences that other people share from their own lives can help the patient in denial realize the true extent of their problems. Group therapies are indeed a better way to make someone realize they have a problem with anger than talking to them about it directly.

Benefits of Group Therapy

The benefits of being a part of a group undergoing therapy for anger are a lot! First of all, it will make you realize that you are not the only one suffering from these problems, and that there are many others who have the same problem just like you. If you have always felt like an outsider - isolated and misunderstood by the people around you, you will find there are many others who have also felt the same.

What can be better than a therapist with academic knowledge trying to be sympathetic with you? When people who have actually been through the same problem tell you they understand!

Listening to stories of how other people's anger has damaged their lives can help you evaluate your situation. If you were worried about how your temper causes you to be rude to people, you might find out how someone has lost multiple jobs in under a year, leaving them unemployed. There is always someone who is in a worse situation than you; hearing their stories might make you feel better than you have felt before, knowing that your life is actually better than you have imagined it to be.

Participants of an anger management group therapy come from a variety of backgrounds, situations and education, of both genders. Although they are very different from each other, they have one thing in common: *anger has damaged their lives.* It may be their careers that have suffered or their relationships – but anger has a way to destroy the things we value the most in our lives. This is true for everyone in the world regardless of the background we come from.

Besides, when you are a part of a group, you have access to thought patterns other than yours. While you or someone in your situation sees a problem from one angle, someone else in a different position but with the same problem can offer a completely different solution. Think of it this way: *if you are having marital problems because of your anger issues, who can help you better?* Someone who neither has anger issues or problems in their marriage? Or someone who has, although a very different life from yours, faced both problems and come out successful?

Joining an Anger Management Group

If you are interested in joining a similar Anger Management group in your locality, ask your physician or your therapist. Both these people will have a good idea of the group therapies available in your area, and help you join the one where you will be most comfortable.

Before joining a group to discuss your anger issues, there are some factors that you need to consider, i.e.

—Whether this is an open group or a closed one. In an open group, anyone can join in at any point of the session. However, if you are not comfortable sharing your stories with strangers on your first meeting, a closed group would be a preferable option. In a closed group, you can continue the whole session with the same people you start with, and over a few weeks, they will feel like friends rather than casual acquaintances.

— Whether you want a small group or a large one. A small group is where the therapist is going to focus on each of the members individually and address their problems; on the other hand, in a large group, you will have a lot of sympathetic ears and lots of novel perspectives.

—Whether you can rely on group therapy alone. If you can't, you can ask for separate one-on-one sessions with the moderator/therapist beside the group sessions.

—Whether you want to share everything. No one will be forcing you to share your deepest and darkest secrets in a group. In fact, no one can force you to share anything. You can attend as a silent spectator if you want to, and talk only when you are comfortable with the other people in the group.

Talking to other sufferers and a moderator in a group

session doesn't sound like much, but it has known to help a lot of people identify their problems.

Cognitive Behavioral Therapy (CBT)

If you are not too enthusiastic about joining a group for discussing your anger issues, the next option is a one-on-one session with your therapist where they can apply several well-researched and effective therapeutical approaches on you. One such approach is the Cognitive Behavioral Therapy technique, or CBT.

CBT is a talk therapy that will mainly work with your thoughts and opinions. That is, what makes you angry and what happens to you in anger – that's what therapists practicing CBT are concerned about. How you behave when angry is just the aftermath of your feelings and will automatically improve when your thought patterns are improved.

Cognitive Behavioral Therapy is an extremely safe treatment that is also used in treating other similar mental distresses, such as anxiety, stress and depression. This therapy can been recommended and declared safe by the National Institute for Health and Care Excellence (NICE) [18] in United Kingdom. In the United States, National Anger Management Association (NAMA) [19] provides training and certification for therapists to practice Cognitive Behavioral Therapy with patients suffering from anger issues.

Therapists all over the world feel comfortable using CBT in treating patients suffering from extreme anger and found it effective.

What is Cognitive Behavioral Therapy?

CBT believes that it is how we see an outsider incident that determines how we will act, not the incident itself. For example, if a person who is always angry wakes up in the morning thinking that this is not going to be a good day, they will spend the whole day getting angry at the smallest provocations. They will be furious if it rains, if they get stuck in traffic, if they bump into someone on the road, or even if the printer at work runs out of ink. They will get angry at everything because that thought has settled into their mind: *everything, all through the day, will go wrong!*

According to Cognitive Behavioral Training, it is our thoughts that determine our behavior. It was Dr. Aaron T. Beck[20] – a graduate from Brown University and Yale Medical School, who first came up with this concept in the 1960s. He was working with a group of patients suffering from depression when he first thought about CBT. He realized that by influencing the thoughts of his patients, he can change their behavior. This was the beginning of Cognitive Behavioral Therapy. From then on, CBT has been used in the treatment of numerous mental and emotional disorders, including anger.

What to Expect in CBT Treatment?

Yes, like other similar therapies, CBT requires you to sit down and talk to a therapist about your feelings, but it is more than that. With this treatment, a therapist takes into account the negative thoughts going on inside a patient's mind and tries to convert them into positive ones. It's what goes on inside our brain to make us angry at the present that's important to the therapist, not what has happened in the past.

Cognitive Behavioral Therapy (CBT) treatments can last for a few weeks, or a few months – depending on your requirements. It is usually a one-on-one session with a therapist you have to be completely honest with about your issues. The therapist will look into your history of outbursts in the recent past and try to determine your triggers. You will talk about your outbursts with your therapist – about how an incident made you feel and why you think you became angry.

A CBT session usually lasts for an hour, and once a week. Between each session, the therapist may give you tasks to complete at home, like homework. Although the tasks would differ based on your condition, there are a few common ones that all therapists prescribe.

Journaling [21]

Journal therapy is a well-recognized technique prescribed for a number of mental disorders, including anger. This is different than simply writing into a journal because here, more focus is given on how you are feeling inside rather than what's happening outside. While writing about your feelings, you can yourself assess why you are angry, and slowly begin to understand your anger. Journal technique is the perfect way for you to know yourself and be honest, reflective and insightful.

Mindfulness [22]

Mindfulness is the art of being present in the moment, rather than thinking about the past or the future. This technique is a great way to pay attention to ourselves – our thoughts, our mind, our sensations, our feelings, as well as our body. Mindfulness has its root in Buddhist ideals, and has been used for centuries as a way for us to control our emotions, instead of being controlled by them.

Relaxation Technique

As described in the previous part of the book, the therapist also prescribes some relaxation techniques to try the next time you get angry. These techniques can be meditation exercise, simple breathing exercise or mindfulness techniques that can calm the mind on the onset of an outburst.

Skill Development

The therapist can also contribute in teaching you some techniques on developing certain skills, especially in the fields you had problems earlier. If you were constantly getting angry because you couldn't communicate well with you teenage children, the therapist will help you with ideas for you to bond well with your children.

Coping Mechanism

A strong coping mechanism is something that many of us don't have inside, which makes it hard for us to deal with a lot of stuff, i.e. loss of a loved one, estrangements and breakups, financial trouble, losing a job, people moving away, etc. Almost all of these things are inevitable in our lives and when we can't cope with them, we get angry. A therapist will help you learn ways to cope up with losses and negative incidents in our life so that we don't get angry when they happen.

These tasks, or homework, are very important in Cognitive Behavioral Therapy, because an hour-long session once a week is not enough to control anger. To make CBT successful, it is important that you are completely honest with your therapist and continue this treatment till the end, and that you follow through all the exercises prescribed by them.

Medication

Although it is not possible to prescribe medication for anger, it is definitely possible to prescribe some for the symptoms that come with anger. Depending on the laws where you live, your therapist will be able to prescribe a few medicines if the symptoms are too extreme, so can your physician.

Some antidepressants are prescribed when a patient suffers from depression after an outburst. Similarly, epilepsy medications are recommended if the outburst lead to a seizure. However, these kinds of medications do not directly affect anger; rather, they help to calm down a person and relax them.

Some anti-allergy and cough medicines can help reduce anxiety – a trait that is common in people who are always in a temper. Therapists sometimes recommend Passion Flower or Chamomile – two herbal supplements that are taken with tea or as medicine that can also reduce anxiety and restlessness.

Please note: *none of these medicines, even the herbal supplements, should be taken without consulting your therapist or physician. This book has only mentioned these medicines as examples;* **this is not a prescription for anger management and should not be taken into consideration. If you believe you can benefit from the use of medication, consult your physician.**

Conclusion

Anger is a part of us – a part which is both good and bad. Although we don't really like the angry part of ourselves, there's no denying that it is also necessary. This is a powerful emotion inside us that we can neither ignore nor show; neither suppress, nor let go. What we can do is to channel our anger to a more productive energy – an energy that we can use to improve our lives!

This book describes everything you need to know about anger – what it is, how it occurs inside us, how to understand the anger within us, and what can it do to us. More importantly, this book deals with how to control anger – not by hiding and burying it deep down, but by channeling it to the right direction. You can do this in two ways: *by yourself or with the help of a professional.* Both ways have been described in this book.

A PERSONAL FAVOR:

If you like this book – and I hope you do – please email me at mmartinez@consejeria.net and let me know your thoughts and how this book helped you.

Blessings!

Bonus Chapter

Relaxation Techniques

Relaxation techniques are neither hard, nor very complex; rather, they are easier than physical exercises and require very little time and no equipment. Even if you have never, ever in your life, tried relaxing, it won't take you more than a few times to master these techniques.

What you do need is some peace and quiet, and 5 minutes to yourself. You can't expect to concentrate on relaxing when there's chaos all around you, the television blaring on full volume and children demanding your attention. Choose a time when there will be no one to disturb you and nothing to distract you. Early in the morning or late at night – around 10 minutes a day, divided into two sessions, is all you need.

This bonus chapter has three simple relaxation techniques for you to try. They are easy, and you can start them anytime you feel like.

Breathing

Yes, we do breathe – all day, 24/7, all through our lives; but, do we ever stop to concentrate on our breaths? This technique will help you – perhaps, for the first time in your life – to focus on your breath and nothing else around you.

Take a seat and make sure you are in a quiet surrounding. It's better if you are outside or near a window, with access to plenty of fresh air. Sit down comfortably and relax your body; close your eyes to start. Now, breath in, with your whole focus on the breathe you are taking. Inhale for as long as you can, filling your lungs with fresh air. Try to feel the oxygen as it travels inside – from your nostril to your lungs. Wait for a second and then exhale, taking as long as you can. Do this a couple of times; don't hurry but take all the time you need.

Your concentration should be completely on your breaths. If your mind is bothered by anything else, especially if something that has recently made you angry or disturbed you, try to push it away. Don't force the thought away – that's not how it works! Whatever it is, don't let that thought bother you for more than a second. Bring your focus back to your breaths and continue. After a while, your mind will automatically clear and you will be able to open your eyes feeling refreshed and energized.

This is a great technique to calm yourself down when you are fearing an outburst. Take a few minutes to yourself, remove yourself from the situation which is infuriating you and practice this technique. You will feel like a completely new person, I guarantee you!

Concentration

This technique is similar to breathing, but still different. For starters, you need to sit down straight – with your posture rigid, your shoulders level and your head upright. Your eyes need to be open and you have to gaze straight ahead. Choose your surrounding well so that you won't be disturbed; your concentration is very important for this technique.

To start, pick up an ordinary object right in front of you. This could be anything – a flower, a ball, a mug or your curtains. Now, concentrate on what you are looking at. Think about the color, the design and how that object looks like to you; try to imagine what it would feel in your hands, the texture and the temperature. Don't think about it too specifically, i.e. don't try to define it or think of its uses for you. Even if it is something you look at every day, try to imagine new aspects of it that you haven't noticed before.

When you are done concentrating on the first object, move to something else. Watch it in the same way, with your whole concentration on it. After a few minutes, you will feel fresher and whatever you were angry about, will be long gone from your mind.

Walking Meditation

This technique requires you to take a walk outside, but even when you are walking, you will be meditating at the same time.

The best time to practice this meditation is when you are angry about something but don't want to show it. Remove yourself from that location for a few minutes and take a walk. It would be better if you can take a stroll outside in the fresh air; if you can't somewhere along a window with a good view is fine.

Take a deep breath and start walking – not too fast and not too slow. Walk as if you are out to enjoy yourself. Look around yourself at the trees, at the flowers, at the birds flying away, and at the sky. Try to calm your mind when you are enjoying a nice stroll outside in the fresh air, with so many beautiful and natural things for you to enjoy.

Watch your legs carefully as you walk. Look at how your legs move up and down when you walk; try to feel your leg when they touch the ground. Concentrate on how the rest of your body moves and how the air feels against your face. Try to feel the sunlight on your skin or the cold air if it is winter. Feel and concentrate on anything that is happening to you and around you, as well as your breath. Do this for a few minutes and you will feel all your worries go away!

Yoga Postures for Stress Relief and Anger Management

Have you ever tried yoga? If you haven't, you should definitely try! There are tons of positions of yoga that are extremely beneficial for both your physical and mental health.

Shavasana/The Corpse Posture

Yes, you read it right!

The Corpse posture is the ultimate relaxation position in yoga, guaranteed to make you feel relaxed and free from stress in a matter of seconds. For this position, you need to lie on your back; your hands should be on the ground beside you, in a relaxed position with your palms facing upwards. Your feet should be together but not touching, relaxed. Close your eyes and breathe naturally.

You will start feeling better almost immediately. It is completely okay to stay in this position for as long as you want to; the corpse position is great to practice breathing, as well.

Salavasana/The Locust Posture

For this posture, you need to lie on your stomach, with a pillow right under your abdomen. Behind the small of your back, lock your fingers together. Take a deep breath and as you do, extend your hands behind you, still locked together. Press your feet and knees on to the floor/bed and hold you head up backwards.

Don't pressure yourself but extend your head and hands as much as you can without feeling pain. Hold and count to 10, then exhale and lower your head. Bring back your hands slowly. Inhale and count to 10 again. Repeat the whole procedure a few times until you start feeling relaxed and happy.

Easy, weren't they? These techniques might not sound like much, but they can work wonders on your mind and body. These three techniques and two yoga postures are enough to bring a huge change to your life, by reducing your anger and making you feel more relaxed than ever.

Try them, and you will know what I am talking about!

ABOUT THE AUTHOR

Dr. Mary Ann Martínez is a Licensed Professional Counselor, and a Marriage, Family and Sex Therapist. She runs a successful private practice in Puerto Rico, where she has been helping individuals, couples, and familiar for more than 20 years. Dr. Martínez is also a Faculty Member and Clinical Specialist of University of Phoenix; as well as an ordained minister of the Church of God Movement (Anderson, IN).

You can contact her at mmartinez@consejeria.net.

Notes

1. Intermittent explosive disorder (sometimes abbreviated as IED) is a behavioral disorder characterized by explosive outbursts of anger and violence, often to the point of rage, that are disproportionate to the situation at hand. The disorder is currently categorized in the *Diagnostic and Statistical Manual of Mental Disorders* (DSM-5) under the "Disruptive, Impulse-Control, and Conduct Disorders" category

2. Mood Treatment Center
   http://moodtreatmentcenter.com

3. Williams, J.E., Paton, C.C., Siegler, I.C., Eigenbrodt, M.L., Nieto, F.J., & Tyroler, H. (2000). Anger Proneness Predicts coronary heart disease risk. *Circulation*, 101, (17).
   http://circ.ahajournals.org/content/101/17/2034.full

4. Mostofsky, E., Penner, E.A., & Mittleman, M.A. (2014). Outburst of anger as trigger of acute cardiovascular events: A systematic review and meta-analysis. *European Heart Journal*, 35,(21).
   https://www.ncbi.nlm.nih.gov/pubmed/24591550

5. Romero-Martínez, A., Lila, M., Vitoria-Estruch, S., & Moya-Albiol, L. (2016). Higgh immunoglobulin A levels mediate the association between high anger

expression and low somatic symptoms in intimate partners violence perpetrators. *Journal of Interpersonal Violence*. 31(4). https://goo.gl/6gZRgc

6. Kubzansky, L.D., Sparrow, D., Jackson, B., Cohen, S., Weiss, S.T., & Wright, R.J. (2006). Angry breathing: A prospective study of hostility and lung function in the normative aging study. *Thorax*, 61(10). https://goo.gl/oqjxjz

7. Generalized Anxiety Disorder (GAD) is an anxiety disorder (defined by the DSM 5) characterized by excessive, uncontrollable and often irrational worry, that is, apprehensive expectation about events or activities. This excessive worry often interferes with daily functioning, as individuals with GAD typically anticipate disaster, and are overly concerned about everyday matters such as health issues, money, death, family problems, friendship problems, interpersonal relationship problems, or work difficulties.

8. Kirchheimer, S. (2003) How stress causes miscarriage. https://goo.gl/R2kxdR .

9. Bullying and rampage school shootings https://goo.gl/jTwtlG

10. Father killed his three young children with a hunting knife after wife told him she was leaving him for her Open University lecturer. https://goo.gl/57221i

11. Mothers Against Drunk Driving (MADD)

http://www.madd.org/

12. People for the Ethical Treatment of Animals (PETA). http://www.peta.org

13. Negative Ions https://goo.gl/Sb1Xe6

14. Sleep preserves and enhance unpleasant emotional memories. https://goo.gl/nY2gZl

15. The fast and the furious: Psychologists figure out who gets road rage and find ways to calm them down. https://goo.gl/UKzp2M

16. Nearly 80 percent of drivers express significant anger, aggression or road rage. https://goo.gl/AurR85

17. Group psychotherapy or group therapy is a form of psychotherapy in which one or more therapists treat a small group of clients together as a group. https://en.wikipedia.org/wiki/Group_psychotherapy

18. National Institute for Health and Care Excellence. https://www.nice.org.uk/

19. National Anger Management Association http://namass.org

20. Aaron T. Beck Psychopathology Research Center. https://aaronbeckcenter.org/beck

21. Journal therapy is a type of writing therapy that focuses on the writer's internal experiences, thoughts

and feelings.
https://en.wikipedia.org/wiki/Journal_therapy

22. Mindfulness is the psychological process of bringing one's attention to the internal and external experiences occurring in the present moment, which can be developed through the practice of meditation and other training.
https://en.wikipedia.org/wiki/Mindfulness

Made in the USA
Lexington, KY
03 March 2019